MISSIONS
A FAMILY AFFAIR

A Study of Biblical Missions

Jack B. Scott

GREAT COMMISSION PUBLICATIONS

7401 OLD YORK ROAD, PHILADELPHIA, PENNSYLVANIA 19126

ISBN 0-934688-15-X

Printed in USA

Published by Great Commission Publications
7401 Old York Road, Philadelphia, Pennsylvania 19126

TABLE OF CONTENTS

Introduction to the Study of Biblical Missions

This is not a study of missionary work today or of the present needs in the missionary force, nor is it a study of the history of missions. Many such works are available and do not need to be duplicated in this study.

This is a study of the biblical concepts of missions taught in God's word. It is an attempt to look at the Scriptures and learn what God planned in the way of missionary activity and how he intended his purposes to be carried out by his people.

So often when we think of the biblical mandate for missions we begin with Matthew 28:18–20, as though going into the world with the gospel message were the starting point of missions. We hope this study will show there is an earlier starting place for missions. There is much in God's word about missions—we cannot afford to ignore it—given long before the Great Commission of Jesus Christ was heard at the end of his earthly ministry. Jesus would have assumed an awareness of these earlier teachings in those who obeyed the Great Commission of Matthew 28. If we ignore those other teachings about missions which are in the Bible we will have an inadequate understanding of the doctrine of missions.

Of course this study can only briefly deal with a few of the passages in God's word given to aid the church in laying hold of God's will in regard to missions. Nevertheless we hope they will point the way to further study and commitment of the church to do missions in God's way with God's zeal.

A look at the table of contents will give the reader some idea of where we are going in this study. Key verses are printed in the table of contents to whet our appetite for learning what the Bible as a whole has to say about missions and the present task of Christ's church.

We have chosen the title *Missions: A Family Affair* deliberately. Missions has to do with families and is to be carried out in the context of families—believing families and church families—as a part of the greatest family: the family of God.

1

A SON'S PRAYER — JOHN 17

In the solitude that only the Son of God could know, Jesus came aside to pray. He had carefully instructed his disciples about the things they could expect after his death—but they didn't believe he was going to die.

Jesus had no one to turn to but his Father in heaven. Only he would understand what Jesus came into the world to do and why he had done all he did.

Read John 17 and answer the following questions:

1. What are some of the things Jesus talked to his Father about concerning his mission into the world?

_____

_____

_____

2. What are some of the things Jesus talked about concerning the mission of those he was leaving behind?

_____

_____

The Beginning of Missions

Before we think further about Jesus' prayer let's give some thought to why Jesus would come at this time to pray to the Father and why he would talk now about his life with the Father before the world was.

We need to look at Ephesians 1:4. This verse is most helpful in getting our orientation into this entire study on missions.

Paul tells us that God chose us in Christ before the foundation of the world so that we should be holy and without blemish before him in love.

Think about that for a moment.

God wanted a people to spend eternity with him—a people who could know and love him and who were fit to dwell in his presence forever, happily.

We know God didn't need such a people, because he has existed from all eternity. He was able to enjoy his life to the fullest without man. But he wanted men to enjoy life with him.

Here is the beginning of missions: God's idea to have a people to live with and enjoy him forever. What kind of people were they to be? Our verse in Ephesians gives some idea of what God expected.

They were to be holy, which means to belong completely (wholly) to God. The people who were to live with God forever were to be his exclusive possession. That means they were set aside for him alone. They were to have a sense of belonging to him, to live for and serve him forever. That's why they are called saints (holy ones) in the Bible.

They were also to be without blemish. How else could they live with God forever? God is perfect, with no flaws, so those who were to spend eternity with him must be that way too. If they had flaws they would not be fit for heaven. If they sinned they couldn't live in his presence for long.

They were to be in his presence (before him). God was not thinking of putting them off on some planet to live isolated from fellowship with him. God's whole concept embraced the idea of a people to live in his presence so they could enjoy him and respond to him and he to them—like a family.

And they were to continue in this relationship by the bond of love. Love was something that existed among the persons of the Trinity. If his creatures, who were to live with him forever, were to fit into the family of God they must learn to love also —love God and love one another.

To accomplish this, God decided it would be done through the work of his Son, Jesus Christ. That's what it means when Paul says he chose us in Christ. He made the determination that we should be what he wanted us to be through the work of his Son.

Jesus' Mission

As we return to John 17 we can see the burden on Jesus, God's Son, when he came into the world. The whole future of those whom God had chosen to spend eternity with him rested on Jesus' faithful carrying out of the Father's will on earth.

Jesus knew he couldn't get any help from his disciples at this time. They were still quite confused about his mission and uncertain even whether it would succeed. How could his death mean success? This was their question.

Jesus knew that only the Father would understand. He had no other to whom he could turn.

In his prayer Jesus talks about his mission from the Father. He particularly mentions that he had finished that mission.

Of course Jesus still had to die on the cross. That was the only way men could ever be without blemish in God's sight. They could not do anything to cleanse their sins away—the Bible had taught this from the beginning. The blood of Jesus Christ alone cleanses us from all sin.

But though Jesus had not yet died and risen from the dead he knew that everything leading up to that saving act had been done. Therefore in talking with the Father he viewed it as accomplished.

Because Jesus had finished his mission he was now thinking about his return to the Father. It had been only about 33 years since he left the Father in heaven. But in many ways this time on earth must have seemed an eternity to Jesus. After all, he knew what he was missing, though his disciples could not know at the time Jesus was praying.

Though he could rejoice in the thought of coming home to the Father, nevertheless Jesus also had his mind very much on those he was leaving behind.

The Unfinished Task

Before we address the things Jesus left for his disciples to do consider the world in which he was leaving them.

Jesus was mindful that the disciples would be left in a hostile world. He knew the world would hate them, because as they had come to know him they were no longer able to be like the world. They didn't fit into the world any more than Jesus did. And Jesus knew what the world was about to do to him.

When Jesus left the world the disciples would be in a world that did not know the Father about whom Jesus had taught. They would be in the very difficult position of seeking to please the Father; but the world, which did not know the Father, would not be interested in their deeds or why they were doing them.

What *was* Jesus leaving his disciples to do on earth?

Jesus could look back and see what he had accomplished on earth in the brief thirty or so years he had been here. And though he had done everything the Father sent him to do there was still much to be done if God was to have that whole people he had chosen.

That meant there must be a continuing work of Jesus to complete his mission. Every one whom the Father had chosen before the foundation of the world had to be called and re-deemed.

Jesus was going back to the Father. He was leaving his disciples behind to complete that work in his strength.

Just as the Father sent him into the world, he was now sending them into the world. They would be bearing his gospel to the nations of the world until the whole people of God had been called. This is missions!

By leaving them Jesus was not deserting them. Right now he prayed not only for them but for those who would believe through their word (vs. 20). This is missions—a people left behind in the world to continue to tell men about Jesus Christ, the only Savior—to call the world to repent and believe in him.

Thus in the prayer of Jesus recorded in John 17 we have the intimate words of the Son lifted to the Father about a plan formed in eternity before the world was created. The prayer was concerned with the carrying out of Jesus' mission to be the one—the only one—through whom men could ever come to the Father and live with him forever.

But the prayer included those left behind as well. They would have a work to do, a mission to the world. All of this was in the Son's prayer to his Father.

The *fact* of a mission has been clearly established, but where do we go to learn of that mission and our responsibility in it?

Where Do We Go from Here?

The answer to this question most usually heard—as it pertains to missions—is that we should get busy, go out to the nations and finish the work Jesus has given us to do. We hear the words "Go therefore," and we get up and go.

But wait: haven't we forgotten something? Whose mission is it in the first place? Not ours, but Jesus'. We need to learn from Jesus before we can plunge into his work. Shouldn't we be interested in how *he* says the mission ought to be carried out—to go into the world to call men to faith in Jesus Christ?

When Jesus saw the multitudes wandering about as lost sheep, what did he say must be done? Read Matthew 9:35–38 and answer the following:

1. What had Jesus been doing?

_____

_____

2. What moved Jesus to concern for the multitudes?

_____

_____

3. How did he describe these multitudes?

_____

_____

4. How did he assess the need?

_____

_____

5. What did he declare to be the way to meet that need?

_____

_____

Jesus went about the cities and villages of the region in which he was ministering. The emphasis of his work was on teaching, preaching and healing. By this he showed his own understanding of the mission on which the Father had sent him. If it had only been to die on the cross he could have completed that in much less than three years.

Before he laid down his life on the cross to pay for our sins he had to gather a people to be God's people, a people saved to carry on the mission when he was gone.

Teaching was at the head of his priorities. It was the way he instituted his public ministry (Matthew 5) and continued to be his chief work among his disciples.

But there were many more to be taught than Jesus could possibly reach in the short span of his public ministry. What was his solution? It was compassion on the multitude—compassion that led him to identify with their need and do something about it.

No doubt as he looked over the multitudes Jesus thought of passages such as Ezekiel 34:5 or Zechariah 10:2. These were God's lost sheep who had to be brought into the fold. They, or among them, were those chosen by God in Christ Jesus. But where were the laborers to bring them in?

Jesus did not say to his disciples, "Get busy and go out there and do whatever you can." No: he said, "Pray therefore the Lord of the harvest, that he send forth laborers into his harvest."

Jesus wanted it clearly understood that he is in charge of his work and it is to be done his way, with those equipped by him, in the way he wants them equipped.

Equipping the saints is very much a part of missions, and if it is neglected the whole work goes amiss.

Jesus spent most of his time teaching and training those he left behind. That ought to give us a clue to how we are to approach the whole work of missions in the church today.

When Jesus rose from the dead and the disciples were gathered around him he opened the Scriptures and began to teach them all things that the Scriptures had to say about himself (Luke 24:27).

Why do you think he did this? Wasn't it to show them that if they were to understand him and his mission they must go to his word and study it and apply it to all they did?

That is in a sense what we are going to try to do in these chapters. We are going to God's word, which teaches about Jesus Christ, and seek to see what Jesus saw as he fulfilled his ministry on earth—as he accomplished the mission given him by the Father.

Review Questions

1. When did missions begin?

   _____

   _____

2. Where did the family concept begin?

   _____

   _____

3. What was Jesus' mission?

   _____

   _____

4. What was the mission Jesus left for his followers?

   _____

   _____

5. What do we learn about priorities in missions from Jesus' example?

   _____

   _____

Discussion Questions

1. What is missions all about?

_____

_____

2. How much interest is there in missions in our church?

_____

_____

3. Is our church showing the right priorities in missions?

_____

_____

4. What are our church's goals for responsibility in missions?

_____

_____

2

A FAMILY PLAN — GENESIS 1, 2

To know our responsibilities in missions, we must begin at the beginning of man—at creation.

When the Lord created man on earth, he made him to be what God had purposed for him before creation.

Read Genesis 1:26–2:25 and answer the following questions:

1. How do we see that God made man holy (belonging to him alone)?

_____

_____

2. How do we see that God made him without blemish?

_____

_____

3. How do we see that God created man to be in his presence (to have fellowship with him)?

_____

_____

_____

4. How do we see that God prepared man to be a loving creature?

_____

_____

Man Created with Purpose

In the last lesson we learned God's plan for man whom he
was to create (Eph. 1:4).

As we look at each part of that verse we see that man, as
created, was the way God purposed him to be.

He made man *to be holy*. Man was made in God's image
and in his likeness. The two terms, image and likeness, do not
mean the same thing.

Image—being made in the image of God—implies that man
is not God but an image of him. This means he belongs to God
but is not God nor can he ever be. Being in the image of God
means that man is not the real thing—not God. It does show
who owns him and to whom he is responsible.

To be in the likeness of God shows that he has the capacity
to reflect the glory of God in his own life. His life, coming
from God, is capable of being like God's life, so far as the creature can be like his creator. He can bear some of the character-

istics of God such as his mercy, grace, slowness to anger, lov-ingkindness, truthfulness, readiness to forgive and unwilling-ness to overlook or ignore sin. All these things are possible with man as a reflection of his maker.

God also made man *without blemish*. We read that when God had finished creation—the whole earth and everything in it—he said that it was very good (Gen. 1:31).

Since God never uses the term "good" lightly (see Matt. 19:17) we are assured that when God saw man as good—*very good*—he was at that time without blemish just as God planned him to be.

It is clear that a fellowship existed between God and Adam from the beginning. God talked with him and gave him certain responsibilities. Adam was able to live on a higher level with God than could any other creature on earth. He was able to hear and respond intelligently to the words of his maker. He was therefore created to be *in the presence of God* and to enjoy fellowship with him from the beginning.

Finally, God made man with the capacity to *love* God and his fellow man. Being in the likeness of God gave him this capacity.

God set up certain circumstances—opportunities for love—in Adam. He was given responsibilities before God, and by obeying God he would show his love. As Jesus later declared to his disciples, "If you love me, you will keep my command-ments" (John 14:15).

Moreover God did not leave Adam alone. He gave him a helper suitable to his needs. In other words the Lord made

Adam with certain needs which could be met only by Eve. This established a situation of love—a relationship between two creatures made in God's likeness.

All these truths, revealed in the opening chapters of man's existence on earth, show that God made man to be all he had purposed him to be in the beginning.

Of great significance is the fact that the Lord, when he made man in this perfect state, established marriage and the home. This tells us that being in a family was from the beginning a part of God's whole purpose for those who would spend eternity with him.

Genesis 2 does not give details of the ideal relationships of love in the home. We have to go to other Scripture to know what God expects in family relationships. But here we see that marriage and the home are built into man's existence, essential to his well-being.

The Family: Man's Top Priority

Read Deuteronomy 24:1–5 and answer the following questions:

1. Why was divorce of the unloved woman allowed?

_____

_____

2. How does this passage show what God thinks about divorce?

_____

_____

_____

3. How does this passage show the priority God set on marriage and the establishment of the home?

_____

_____

Jesus was confronted by his enemies with this passage from
Deuteronomy (Matt. 19:7-9). They wanted to justify their
own practice of divorce and knew Jesus was opposed to their
divorces.

They thought Moses' writings justified their setting aside
any wife they did not like and marrying another. But Jesus
showed that the passage taught the opposite.

He pointed out that the writing of divorcement was _not_
given for the benefit of the husband who wanted to get a new
wife or be rid of his old one. It was written to protect the unloved and abused wife whose husband treated her with cruel-
ty. He said it was given by Moses because of the hardness of
their hearts.

A careful reading of the passage shows that, while it allows
the unloved wife to remarry after divorce, it does not allow the
husband to remarry. He can't even remarry her once she has
been given to another!

But the clincher in the whole passage is found in verse 5.

There God shows marriage and the family to be so important it ought to take priority over anything else the husband does. Establishing his own family should be more important to him than going to war—even more important to the *nation* than his going to war. It is also more important than his job. A husband shows his wife and family are top priority by spending a whole year at home seeking to cheer his wife—showing love to her and seeking to meet her needs.

That is undoubtedly what God had in mind when he made man male and female—two lives to become one life in order to produce more life.

The Family: A Community of Subjection

Read Ephesians 5:21–6:4 and answer the following:

1. Why should we begin this passage at verse 21?

_____

_____

2. How does the wife show her subjection to her husband?

_____

_____

3. How does the husband show his subjection to his wife?

_____

_____

4. How do children show their subjection to their parents?

_____

_____

5. How do parents show their subjection to their children?

_____

_____

There is much in the passage which we cannot deal with in this study. Our purpose is to note the *context* of subjection that is absolutely necessary for a family to be what the Lord intended from the beginning.

Willing subjection to one another is a major way people show their love for one another. That's why Paul, as he begins this passage on family relationships, begins with the verse stating: "Subject yourselves to one another in the fear of Christ." Here "fear" means loving obedience.

Wives subject themselves to their husbands as to the Lord. They recognize the Lord has made the husband the spiritual head of the home and its leader. They respect God's decision. As the church is subject to Christ, therefore, they are subject to their husbands as head of the family.

Husbands subject themselves to their wives in reflection of the love Christ had for the church. He loved the church and gave himself up for it, to bring it to its full potential. Husbands are to do the same for their wives.

Children show their subjection to their parents by obedience to them, in accord with God's own arrangement of the family so that children would be blessed as they honored their parents. God set parents over them to train and prepare them for life and service in his Kingdom.

Likewise parents subject themselves to their children by setting aside their own desires and pleasure to bring up their children in the nurture and admonition of the Lord. This takes a lot of time and work with children—a realization that their children have needs which only they can supply—if their children are to meet their full potential of service to God.

This gives some idea of what God from the beginning expected to happen in the family.

But it didn't work that way for long because of man's sin.

Sin and the Reconstruction of the Family

We don't know what would have happened had man not sinned. The fact is that he did sin and so the Lord had to re-create in the image of his Son those who would spend eternity with him.

When man sinned he was no longer fit for heaven. Read Genesis 3:1–15 and answer the following:

1. How did man fail to remain holy?

_____

_____

2. How did he fail to remain without blemish?

_____

_____

3. How did he fail to remain in God's presence?

_____

_____

4. How did he fail to show love to God and to his wife?

_____

_____

5. How did God purpose to redeem man and restore him to his original purpose?

_____

_____

We note that man failed to remain holy when he no longer acknowledged God in his life. Tempted by Satan, he chose to set aside God's word and follow his own pleasure, and he fell from holiness (belonging to God): he rebelled against God.

In his fall Adam showed himself no longer to be without blemish. He immediately began to have evil thoughts and fled from the presence of God—a sinner in trouble with God. He could no longer live in God's presence and feared even the voice of God, which he had been created to enjoy. His love broke down as well: he disobeyed God out of a lack of love and began to mistreat his wife, accusing her for his own failures.

The family itself was threatened, for Adam refused to take the spiritual leadership God had given him. Though he was present when his wife was being tempted he allowed her to make the spiritual decisions for the two of them, abdicating his spiritual responsibility of leadership.

And there it would have remained—man a failure and without any hope of being what God purposed him to be—except that God intervened.

Why did he do this? Because his plan from the beginning was to have a people to be his forever. He would not be frustrated in that purpose—not by man, not by Satan.

Verse 15 has long been recognized as the first gospel promise, the first step in God's plan to call out of sinful humanity a people for himself.

He chose to do so in the context of the family. Out of the seed of sinful men God would raise up a Seed for himself which would ultimately triumph over Satan and his seed. This is the promise of the gospel. The carrying out of that promise is missions: the reaching out into all humanity to establish a people of God, calling people from the family of Satan to the family of God.

Thus from the fall of man emanate two families instead of the one family of God. Genesis 3:15 speaks of the woman and her seed and Satan and his seed. All through Scripture these two families (God's and Satan's) live in the world side by side, and will until the end of time.

From the woman would eventually come, in a family, the Seed who would conquer Satan: Jesus Christ.

We see that it is in the context of the family that God intends to work to carry out his purpose to have a people forever.

Therefore the family, to this day, continues—in the purpose of God—to have a major role in establishing the people of God —missions.

Review Questions

1. What does it mean to be created in God's image?

_____

_____

2. What does it mean to be created in God's likeness?

_____

_____

3. What part does subjection play in a strong Christian family?

_____

_____

4. How did the first human family fail to be God's people?

_____

_____

5. What did God do to revive the family?

_____

_____

Discussion Questions

1. How is the human family like God's eternal family?

_____

_____

2. What does the family have to do with missions?

_____

_____

3. How do families work together in our church?

_____

_____

4. How do family problems affect the work of our church?

_____

_____

3

ONE MAN'S FAMILY — GENESIS 18

It should not surprise us that when God began to gather his people on earth he began with one man's family.

Of course, before Abraham there were other believers and other families of believers. From Genesis 4–11 mention is made of faithful men such as Abel, Enoch, Noah and his sons, to name a few.

But it is evident that through none of these did a continuing people of God develop. From Joshua we ascertain that the immediate ancestors of Abraham (or Abram as he was first called) were pagans (Josh. 24:2). God clearly began to build the church in the world (the continuing visible presence of a people of God) with one man, Abraham, and his family.

Abraham's Faith

The focus of our attention in this lesson will be on Genesis 18:19.

First, a few words about Abraham.

From Genesis 12 we learn how God uniquely intervened in the life of Abraham, calling him away from his pagan family to follow the Lord. He promised to bless all the nations of the world through him (Gen. 12:3).

At this point Abraham's faith was evident as he followed where the Lord led him (12:4). The writer of Hebrews declares that this act of going was an act of faith in the Lord (Heb. 11:8, 9).

In Genesis 15 we learn that Abraham lived by faith in God. When the Lord promised him a multitude of seed as the stars of heaven he believed in the Lord and it was reckoned to him for righteousness (15:6; cf. Rom. 4:1–5).

Abraham's trust in God to fulfill his promise of a countless seed is the starting point in our understanding of how God began to work in this one man's family.

The Environment of Abraham's Family

Read Genesis 18:16–21 and answer the following questions:

1. What is the context in which the Lord began to talk to Abraham about his desires for him and his family?

_____

_____

2. What does the condition of Sodom and Gomorrah tell about our world today?

_____

_____

Even before Isaac was born God began to talk to Abraham about what he expected of his seed. He did so in the context of the impending judgment on Sodom and Gomorrah—cities of the world dedicated not to God but to their own pleasure.

We noted in the last lesson that after the fall of man two families developed on earth: one natural, from natural birth; the other supernatural, by the grace and will of God. Scripture describes them as the children of Satan and the children of God.

It is clear from the context of Genesis 18 that the children of Satan by this time had established themselves strongly in the world. Worldly cities like Sodom and Gomorrah were impressive enough to attract Lot, Abraham's nephew, to seek his fortune there.

But the cities of this world do not please God. Sodom and Gomorrah were destroyed, as we read in Genesis 19, and Lot lost most of his family there. Lot's experience stands as a warning to us.

The dangerous influence of Sodom and Gomorrah on Abraham's family has much to do with us today.

Scripture shows that believers always live in a hostile world which is continually seeking to conform them to its own ways of living and thinking. The threat to Lot and his family, living in Sodom, is not an isolated case.

The psalmist describes the way of the blessed as a way that does not follow the counsel of the wicked or the way of sinners or the position of scoffers (Ps. 1:1).

Paul similarly says, "Be not fashioned according to this world" (Rom. 12:2).

These two verses warn that God's children are constantly bombarded by the influence of the world, which seeks to conform us to its ways and standards.

We need only look at the barrage of advertisements, books and TV shows to realize how great and pervasive this worldly influence is in our society—setting before us evil standards of living and enticing us to lust for the things of this world.

Even on the evening news and in our newspapers we are constantly reminded of the desirability of the "good life" which the world is selling.

Not only we as parents but our children also live daily in such a context that cries out, loud and clear, the ways of the world: the gospel of Satan.

Peter reminds us that the overthrow of Sodom and Gomorrah remains an example of how in the end all the world will be overthrown, destroying all the ungodly seed of Satan—all unbelievers (2 Pet. 2:6–9).

It is significant that God began to talk to Abraham about his family in such a context. It is like Peter after Pentecost, calling his hearers to save themselves from a crooked generation (Acts 2:40). And this is what missions is all about—calling a people out of a world under judgment into the family of God by faith in Jesus Christ. Unless they come out they will be judged as those of Sodom and Gomorrah. Abraham and his family surviving and then being the means of others coming to the Lord before it is too late—this too was what missions is all about.

In Genesis 18:19 we have the first great commission clearly enunciated in Scripture. It is given to a believing family out of which eventually came the whole church of Jesus Christ. It is vital that we give heed to this commission of God to Abraham, for it is given to our families as well.

Teaching: The First Defense against the World

"For I have known him, to the end that he may command his children and his household after him."

The Lord declares he has known Abraham. This means that God chose Abraham to be a part of his family. Now he appoints him to teach his household what the Lord wants his children to know as they live in the world.

Scripture teaches that the word of God is the only true defense against the world. If we and our children are to resist being conformed to his world then we must be faithfully taught the will of God: his word.

This is evident as we return to Psalm 1. After stating negatively that the righteous are blessed because they do not walk in the way of the ungodly, the psalmist declares that the delight of the righteous is in the law (teachings) of the Lord. He meditates on God's word day and night. That alone enables the believer to withstand the world's influence and be molded in accord with the will of God.

Paul too in Romans 12, after warning against conformity with this world, challenges the readers to be transformed by the renewing of their minds, so that they may prove what is the good and acceptable and perfect will of God (Rom. 12:2).

But how does God intend for parents to command their children?

Read Deuteronomy 6:4–9 and answer the following:

1. What must be in the hearts of instructing parents?

_____

_____

2. How are God's words to be taught to their children?

_____

_____

After the Lord had begun to reveal his word to Israel, the family of Abraham, he instructed parents in the way they are to train their children.

First, parents must love the Lord. This enables them to subject themselves to their children's spiritual needs and give the time and effort to teaching them his will. If they do not have God's love in their hearts they'll not be able to train their children to live in this world for the Lord.

But even though they love the Lord they must also love his word and spend sufficient time to understand it. It must be in their hearts, not simply in a book gathering dust in their homes.

Finally they must teach God's word diligently to their children. But what does this mean?

This word actually means "teach them penetratingly." He shows us how.

We must not suppose that merely teaching words to our children is enough. If we do not teach them in such a way that it will sink in (penetrate) then it will avail nothing.

But how do we do that?

We must not only have the word in our own heart and teach it to our children but we must live it daily. That word must be so much a part of our lives that it is evident to our children that we are living by it when we rise in the morning, when we go out to our work, when we return from our work and as we go to bed in the evening.

It must be so much a part of our lives that it is evident to our children that God's word guides all that our hands do and all the plans of our life as we leave our homes to go out into the world.

Believing parents must give the best of their lives to teach their children that God's word is the front line of defense against the inroads of the world into the home and into the church. It is certain that, if the world enters our homes and has its way in our lives, it will surely enter into our churches as well.

Living: First Testimony to the World

"That they may keep the way of the Lord, to do righteousness and justice."

The believing family is the greatest testimony that there is a people of God in the world because they have learned to keep the way of the Lord. Such a people, though in the world, do not live as the world does but are living proof of the power of God's gospel.

As children in the home come to believe in Jesus Christ they are able, in turn, to live in a way that pleases him. Faith comes by hearing the word of Christ, and faith produces lives that glorify him before the world.

The terms "righteousness" and "justice" are the Old Testament terms that describe the expected fruit of a faithful life and bear testimony that God has been working in that life.

The psalmist describes the believer as one who bears fruit in his season (1:3). In the Old testament that fruit is righteousness and justice; in the New Testament it includes such fruit as love, joy, peace, longsuffering, gentleness, goodness, faithfulness, meekness and self-control (Gal. 5:22, 23)—fruit of the Spirit.

Satan and his world have no defense against such lives, which are a testimony that cannot be silenced by the world.

Growing: First Offensive into the World

"To the end that the Lord may bring on Abraham that which he has spoken of him."

What has the Lord spoken of Abraham?

In Genesis 15:5 the Lord promised, in the context of Abraham's faith, that he would increase his seed as the stars of the heaven.

Read Romans 4:13–17 and answer the following:

1. Who are the true seed of Abraham promised by God?

———————————————————————————

2. How do we all come to be in the family of Abraham?

Paul's point here is that the promise to Abraham that he would have a multitude of seed was not fulfilled by the nation of Israel. It was fulfilled by a multitude of people from all nations who had the same kind of faith as Abraham (cf. Rom. 9:6-8).

It is not enough for us to be born into a believing family. We must come to the Lord in faith; we must be taught by his word; we must begin to live for his glory.

God said to Abraham that, by raising his own children to be a strong and faithful family of believers, he would be building the church of God on earth.

The individual families of believers today are the building blocks of the church. From them children go forth to live in the world and take the gospel to the world. They are the front line of missions in the church, and without them the church will fail in its mission.

It is imperative therefore that, in contemplating any church's mission program for Christ, the family and its instruction in God's word receive top priority. Christian (biblical) education is the means to a more faithful mission into the world. Short cuts taken by any church become dead ends!

Review Questions

1. How was Abraham's faith shown?

_____

_____

2. Describe the world in which Abraham lived.

_____

_____

3. What is the first defense of the church against the world?

_____

_____

4. What is the first testimony of the church to the world?

_____

_____

5. What was the Great Commission to Abraham and his family?

_____

_____

Discussion Questions

1. What are some ways a Christian family shows its faith to the world today?

2. Describe the threats from the world to Christian families today.

3. How can the church help Christian families stand against the world?

4. Discuss ways that families in your church can reach the world around them.

4

ROOTS AND MISSIONS — ISAIAH 6

God never said it would be easy for his family to live in this world and, at the same time, reach out to the nations of the world to call other people to him. This fact was certainly clear to the prophet Isaiah.

Isaiah relates the experience of his call from God. He tells how he became aware of God forgiving his sin, but he tells more. He tells us how God called him to go where the Lord would send him, to deliver God's message to unbelievers of the world (Is. 6:1-8).

He readily volunteered to do this for the Lord who had just made salvation known to him. But understandably he wanted to know more about that ministry.

The Lord didn't paint a pretty picture. Isaiah was not encouraged to expect that many of those to whom he spoke would take him seriously. Most would not understand his message.

As a result his ministry would bring many into condemnation, not salvation. That was a glum prospect to say the least.

Isaiah wanted to know how long such a ministry of proclamation to the world would last. That answer was not encouraging either. It would last until the day of judgment on Israel, the nation to which he was sent (6:9–12).

That did not mean Isaiah would be a failure—far from it. He would be the means of preserving a remnant, a holy seed that would arise out of a world under judgment, becoming the people of God (6:13).

Later in his prophecy Isaiah talked about Immanuel (God-with-us) who was to be born of a virgin (7:14), and of one who is to be named Wonderful, Counselor, Mighty God, Everlasting Father, Prince of Peace—the heir of David's throne (9:6, 7).

Finally, in 11:1, he spoke of one coming out of the stock of Jesse, a branch out of his roots that will bear fruit.

All these verses are speaking of the same thing: the birth of God's own Son, to be the root (vine) which supports branches, which bear fruit (cf. John 15). Note how closely this agrees with Ephesians 1:4—a people chosen *in Christ* to be God's people forever, holy and without blemish, in God's presence, in a bond of love.

Isaiah was one sent by God to claim such people out of the world.

The prophet understood he was not to expect all to whom he brought the message to believe. Many would not, and would be condemned by God. But a remnant would believe—making it all worthwhile.

Isaiah was not the only one who would bear God's message of redemption. As he begins his prophecy he tells of many going out and bringing back a great multitude of the redeemed.

Nations Flowing to Zion

Read Isaiah 2:2–4 and answer the following questions:

1. What is so unusual about nations flowing to a high mountain?

_____

_____

2. Who goes out to the nations to invite them to come to Zion?

_____

_____

3. What goes out with the message-bearers?

_____

_____

4. What is God doing as they go out and call the nations?

_____

_____

5. What is the result in those who respond positively to the invitation?

_____

As Isaiah envisions the latter days—the period from the time of Christ until the end of human history on earth—he sees a marvelous thing happening.

The nations, like rivers, will flow. But, unlike rivers, they will flow up to the highest of mountains, the mountain of God's house—also called Zion in this text. To flow upwards to God's house they must be aided by the power of God. Natural men, like natural rivers, flow downward, not upward.

How will this happen? By many people, such as Isaiah, being sent into the nations to invite others to come with them to the Lord. They are invited to come and learn God's ways and to learn to walk in his paths.

Does this sound familiar? Is it not exactly what Abraham was told to do in his own family? Isaiah explains that the instruction of God's word would go from Jerusalem (home) out to the nations of the world.

How like the Great Commission Isaiah's passage is! Go therefore and make disciples of all the nations . . . teaching them to observe all things whatsoever I commanded you . . . beginning in Jerusalem (Matt. 28; Acts 1:8).

The action of God, simultaneous with the effort of those he sends into the nations, will be to judge between the nations and decide between many peoples. It does not say that Isaiah or any other who is sent will do the judging or deciding. They will be declaring. But as they declare God's word and teach it God will call his own out of the masses who have heard.

Those chosen by God will no longer be citizens of the nations primarily, but of God's kingdom. This will be evident by the change in their relationship with God—from enmity to peace. As Paul later said, having been justified by faith we have peace with God through our Lord Jesus Christ (Rom. 5:1).

Those saved will use their lives not for warring against God but for growing and cultivating the fruit of the Spirit that God desires to see in his children.

It should not be difficult to see that this prophecy of Isaiah has to do with the great commission of the Lord taught earlier to Abraham (see our previous chapter).

As the Lord taught in Acts 1:8 his people are to carry the witness of the gospel of Jesus Christ to the nations of the world—beginning in Jerusalem . . . beginning in their own families!

A real problem with our view of missions is that we often think of missions as going to other nations—period. But missions begins in our own homes, and from there to our own nation and from there to the nations of the world.

The Bible does not make the distinctions we so often make: Christian education in the home; home missions; foreign missions. In the Bible it is all one mission: Christ's mission for his church into the world around us.

Much of Isaiah's prophecy concerns the mission of God's

people into the world. We will look at just one other chapter: Isaiah 43.

The Mission—Phase One: Redemption

Read Isaiah 43:1–4 and answer the following questions:

1. Describe the God who speaks here.

_____

_____

2. What has he done for his people?

_____

_____

3. How does he describe his watchcare over them?

_____

_____

4. What does it mean, he gives Egypt, Ethiopia and Seba as their ransom?

_____

_____

5. Why has he chosen them over others?

_____

The Lord describes himself to his people as their creator, former, redeemer and savior. The terms "creator" and "former" are used in the first two chapters of Genesis to describe the making of man.

Creating man is in conjunction with the creation of all other creatures. But *forming* man has to do with God's special care in forming each individual, as a potter forms a vessel from the clay with his own particular design and purpose in mind. Compare Genesis 1:27 and 2:7.

The terms "redeemer" and "savior" are also related. To redeem is to buy back that which is presently lost. To save is more general: to save from the normal judgment expected.

God called his people and claimed them as his own. They will prove to be steadfast. They will endure, tested by fire and water. While others will perish, they will not. This is why he says: "Others will be given as ransom in their place."

And why this favorable treatment shown those who are saved? Scripture never gives a reason beyond the love of God. He regards them as precious in his sight. We look in vain for any other reason.

The right view of biblical missions depends on our understanding how God works. He does not pick the best of men for his people. There are no such people.

Instead he sets his love on some for reasons beyond our ability to understand, and *makes* them the best of men. He does all that is necessary to redeem and save them. This is the meaning of God's grace.

We are not to rule out any as ineligible for God's salvation. We do not know, nor is it our business to know, who are the redeemed. That's why our mission is to proclaim the gospel to *every* nation. God knows and will reach all of his through us.

The Mission—Phrase Two: Bring My Sons and My Daughters from the End of the Earth

Read Isaiah 43:5-7 and answer the following:

1. Why will the mission of God's people into the world succeed?

_____

_____

2. From what parts of the earth will the seed of God be gathered?

_____

_____

3. How inclusive is this?

_____

_____

To go, preach and succeed in such a difficult mission sounded like an impossible task to Isaiah when God first called him.

It always sounds impossible for the people of God—so greatly outnumbered in the world—to succeed in their mission.

Our mission is not to change the world or make the world better or win the whole world to be in the church. We might think we could succeed in that, given enough time.

Our mission is a lot harder. It is to reach *every one* of those whom God has chosen and call them to faith in Jesus Christ. We must not miss a single one.

Impossible for us? Yes—but not for Christ. In Isaiah as well as in the Great Commission of Matthew 28 he promises: "I am with you." That alone will make the difference between success and failure of our generation of believers—or any other generation in the past or future.

Missions—Phase Three: You Are My Witnesses

Read Isaiah 43:8–13 and answer the following:

1. Who in this world is going to tell of God and his salvation if not his people?

_____

2. Of whom are we witnesses?

_____

3. What alternative do men have as a savior if not the Lord?

_____

_____

4. Who can deliver out of God's hand?

_____

_____

5. Who can hinder God's work of redemption?

_____

_____

Isaiah envisions the whole world gathered together—those who have eyes to see and do not see and ears to hear and do not hear—and asks if any from among that motley crew can bring a message to the world that will save men—a message of truth.

Of course no such message from the world can save, because there is no saving truth in the world. That's why we, who are his people, must be his witnesses in the world. There's no one else to do it.

There is no other god like our God with a similar message of salvation that is true. Satan, the god of this world, does have a message and a gospel, but it is full of lies—though most of the world believes and follows these lies.

But if God is the only savior he is also the only judge. No one can deliver men out of his hand. No higher court exists: he is the final authority, and those who do not believe in him are condemned already.

Do you believe that? Do you believe that all who do not believe in Jesus are condemned to hell? The Bible says they are. That's why our witness is so vital to the world, whether the world recognizes it or not. And so Christ's mission is *our* mission and must have top priority in our families, in our churches and in our world.

If no one can deliver sinners out of God's hand, it is also true that no one can hinder the Lord in his purpose to call his people from the world to himself through his witnesses.

He will work and none can hinder his work. That is his promise in Isaiah 43, and throughout Scripture, as we shall see.

This great passage from Isaiah's prophecy should convince us that the Lord has been teaching his church about missions for a long time—long before Jesus came into the world.

Isaiah isn't the only Old Testament prophet who saw this mission. We'll look at Daniel's message next.

Review Questions

1. What was difficult about Isaiah's call?

_____

_____

2. What is strange about nations flowing to Mount Zion?

_____

_____

3. How do we often view missions as different from the way Scripture does?

_____

_____

4. What three phases of missions does Isaiah discuss in chapter 43?

Discussion Questions

1. How does our task compare to Isaiah's in his day?

_____

_____

2. How is our church involved in instructing the nations to-day?

_____

_____

3. How are the tasks of world missions, home missions and Christian education related?

_____

_____

4. What are the problems related to our believing that all who do not believe in Jesus Christ are condemned to hell?

_____

_____

5

SAINTS OF THE MOST HIGH—
DANIEL 1, 2, 3, 12

The book of Daniel is the most missionary-oriented book in the Old Testament, perhaps in the Bible. It's about the children of God living and working in the pagan world, bearing witness of the Lord to unbelievers.

God's Children in the Kingdom of the World

Read Daniel 1 and answer the following questions:

1. Why do you think Daniel and his friends were placed in the school of Babylon?

_____

_____

2. How did Daniel and his friends counter the influence of the world in their lives?

_____

_____

_____

3. How did Daniel and his friends succeed in the kingdom of the world?

_____

_____

It was not the desire of Daniel and his friends to live in a pagan land and be forced to receive a pagan education. Nevertheless, finding themselves in this circumstance, they sought to use that opportunity for the glory of their Lord.

Clearly Nebuchadnezzar desired to mold their lives to suit his own purposes. They were given the best of learning in Babylon, but it was secular. Note how he had their Hebrew names changed so that they no longer contained God's name but the names of the gods of Babylon.

Daniel could do little about any of this. He was physically under the control of pagans. Nevertheless he (and presumably the other three Hebrew children with him) purposed in his heart to honor God.

The Lord was pleased with their commitment. He caused them to be favored by the pagans who controlled them so that they were able to honor their God by rejecting the pleasures of the world. It was the only way they could show they were not of the world, though in the world.

Because of their faithfulness, the Lord enabled them to live better on their meager diet than all their rivals in the school of Babylon.

In the end the four were given knowledge from God which

far exceeded the world's knowledge and enabled them to serve well the needs of the pagan government.

All this should help us see that, as God's servants in the world, we are like Daniel. We are all living in a pagan world under pagan governments.

In order to survive under such conditions, it's imperative that we be trained to love the Lord our God with all our heart, soul and mind. That training, as we have seen, comes best in the believing home.

Daniel and his companions are an excellent example of how the believing home equips God's children to be true missionaries to the world. They were clearly the product of home training in the way of the Lord.

Basic Christian education must be in the home, as we have seen. If that is omitted our children will not be able to resist the influence of the world and serve the Lord.

Christian schools can supplement that training but cannot take its place. God has put the responsibility squarely in the hands of believing parents, in the home.

Daniel and his friends were called to serve a pagan government—a very secular job. But they turned that secular job into full-time Christian service, dedicating themselves and their work to the glory of their God. This is missionary work at its best (cf. Eph. 6:5-7; Col. 3:22-25).

The Kingdom of God among the Kingdoms of the World

Read Daniel 2:28-45 and answer the following questions:

1. How did Daniel glorify his God before the pagan world?

_____

_____

2. What was the difference between the kingdoms of this world and the kingdom of God?

_____

_____

3. What does Daniel's interpretation have to say about the present world?

_____

_____

The early part of this chapter tells of Nebuchadnezzar's dream. It troubled him greatly. The failure of his own advisors to interpret the dream gave opportunity for Daniel to glorify God before the pagan world.

Daniel took the occasion to honor his God. He would not take credit for his knowledge. He honored God instead.

As he interpreted the dream, he declared the real meaning of human history.

For those of the world, such as the king and his successors, history was a series of kingdoms rising and falling—wars and rumors of wars. But from God's perspective human history was the establishing of the kingdom of God among the kingdoms of this world.

Those who set their hope in the kingdoms of this world would see those hopes dashed. There's no hope in men's efforts in this world. All hope rests in what God is doing through his kingdom among the kingdoms of this world.

We can learn from this that, today as well, the world sees the real purpose of human history to be the exaltation of man. Like Daniel we must see and interpret to the world the real purpose of all human history: the building of God's kingdom.

We are on a rescue mission to call men out of the kingdoms of the world into the kingdom of our Lord. Only believers know the true purpose of God in history. It is not written in the world's history books or taught in its schools. It must come as we know God and his word and are bold to proclaim it.

Who's in Charge?

Since God's people in the world are outnumbered and their purposes run counter to the purposes of the world, they can expect continuing conflict with the world. Such was the case with the three companions of Daniel.

Read Daniel 3 and answer the following questions:

1. How does this chapter reveal the folly of the world?

_____

_____

2. How does it reveal the enmity of the world?

_____

_____

3. What enabled the three Hebrew children to withstand the pressure of the world?

_____

_____

When the king began thinking of himself in the place of God, God's enemies took the occasion to try to destroy the children of God in Babylon.

Though Nebuchadnezzar knew the benefit these young men were to his kingdom his own vain pride and worldly mind-set blinded him so that he put them in the position of having to choose between him and their God.

That happens today as we work in the unbelieving world. Our faith will be challenged and we will face what these three men faced: the choice of serving God or serving men.

They remained faithful because they understood that the one in control was not Nebuchadnezzar but God—their God.

Threatened with death, they made clear to the king they were not accountable to him above God.

They were sure God *could* deliver them from death. But they did not know whether that was his will. They did not say

God would deliver them from death—he might desire that they die for his glory. However, they knew that whether they lived or died was in God's hands, not man's. What happened to them was God's decision.

On the basis of the will of God as they knew it—that which he had revealed in his written word—Shadrach, Meschach and Abednego refused to bow down to the image and worship it. Faced with a choice, they subjected themselves to death as ordered by the king rather than choose to bow to his image. They were subject to the king, choosing the alternative he gave them: death.

We can learn much from this about missionary service.

God's word teaches us to be subject to the powers that be (Rom. 13:1-7). But there is a power above the powers of this world.

We also must be willing to be in subjection to the government under which we live and to pay the penalty for our stand. We are not to cry out against it. See the example of the early believers in Acts (5:29; 12:1-5).

Our mission is not to resist the laws of the land but to do what God's word teaches and be willing to take the consequences. Our mission is to proclaim God's word, not try to change the world!

This does not mean we are to remain silent when kings and peoples do not do what is right. Daniel did not hesitate to exhort the king to break off his sins by doing what was right and showing mercy to the poor (4:27). But he did it at risk to himself and did not resist the government under which he lived.

There is much here for the church today. It is increasingly popular to demonstrate and resist the laws of the land; but that is the world's way, not God's.

What Ought We to Be Doing?

Read Daniel 12 and answer the following questions:

1. How does Daniel describe human history?

_____

_____

2. How does he describe the end of human history?

_____

_____

3. Who are the truly wise in the world and what will they be doing during human history?

_____

_____

4. What will the world be doing in the same period?

_____

_____

Michael the archangel is identified as the one who aids God's people in their battle with Satan (Dan. 10:13, 21; Jude 9; Rev. 12:7). According to the latter verse he is the one who casts out Satan from God's presence so that the devil is confined to the earth.

Our main concern is the time of trouble described in Daniel 12:1.

Jesus described human history in similar terms (Matt. 24:5–14). Though a time of hardships it is also the time God's people are being delivered from the world into the kingdom of God—all whose names are written in the book (the Lamb's book of life, Rev. 13:8).

The climax to human history is the separating of God's children from Satan's forever: everlasting life or everlasting contempt.

What are God's children to be doing until that final day comes?

They will be turning many to righteousness—mission work. They will shine forth their light on earth so that God in heaven may be glorified (Matt. 5:16).

It will not be easy, as we have seen. The world will try to break the people of God and seek their destruction but they will not succeed, as Nebuchadnezzar did not succeed against Daniel and his three friends.

The world and human history will witness many who make themselves pure in Christ their savior while the rest go on doing wickedly in the world until time runs out.

Daniel has reminded us that those who are wise—who take seriously the word of God—will understand their mission in the world and dedicate their lives to turning many to the righteousness that is offered by faith in Jesus Christ.

Review Questions

1. How did Daniel show his biblical training?

_____

_____

2. What does Nebuchadnezzar's dream teach about the world and God's church?

_____

_____

3. How did the three friends of Daniel witness?

_____

_____

4. What does God expect his children to be doing in the world?

_____

_____

Discussion Questions

1. How do parents today prepare their children for the secular world?

_____

_____

_____

2. How can we witness to governments without becoming involved in their missions?

_____

_____

3. What's wrong (right?) with Christians becoming involved
   with non-Christians to oppose laws of the land?

_____

_____

4. How can we today be subject to governments we don't like
   and yet maintain a faithful witness?

_____

_____

6

NATIONS RAGING — PSALM 2

If Daniel is the missionary book of the Old Testament then the book of Psalms is surely the missionary's hymnal. Not just a few of the psalms pertain to missions: the entire psalter is concerned with the missionary (child of God) in a hostile world as God's witness.

The first two psalms introduce us to the content of the entire book and enable us to understand the various topics dealt with in the psalter as they pertain to the missionary's life in the world.

The Two Destinies of Mankind

Read Psalm 1 and answer the following questions:

1. What is the attitude of God's child (the blessed) toward this world and its influence?

_____

_____

2. How is the child of God (the righteous one) able to withstand the influence of this world and stand for the Lord?

_____

_____

_____

3. How do the righteous and the wicked contrast in their lives?

_____

_____

4. What makes the difference between the way of the righteous and the way of the wicked?

_____

_____

This psalm deals with the contrast between the righteous and the wicked. The disadvantage of the righteous is that he has to live out his days in a world favorable to the wicked, not to him. As we saw in God's instructions to Abraham it is vital that the child of God be taught the Lord's way from earliest times in order that he not be lured by the ways of the world to sin against God.

He has to cope with the counsel of the world which continually broadcasts to men the thoughts and goals of the world. It is called the counsel of the wicked.

He also has to cope with the ways of the world, living in the midst of a people who enjoy the things of this world, its treasures and rewards. To gain those rewards he would have to go the way of the world—play the game by their rules—or be left out so far as the world is concerned.

And since the world eventually becomes negative and cynical about life he must resist the scoffers in the world who sit back and degrade this life as though nothing of value is here. He must remember that *he* is here for a good purpose: to call men out of the world to the Lord.

But how can the child of God, surrounded by so much evil, successfully resist the world's assessment of things and move in a way that pleases his Lord? By meditating continually on God's word (law). For the believer this is a delight, because he knows that only in what the word of God has to say can he find anything that will satisfy him.

When you consider how much of the average person's time is given to attention to the world's propaganda (Satan's gospel) compared with the amount of time given to serious study of God's word, it is staggering.

Add up all the time spent before the TV and reading the magazines and newspapers of the world, together with the books, radio, advertisements and other messages which bombard us daily. Add to that our own idle time spent in meaningless conversation and meaningless pursuits every day.

Now compare that to the amount of time we spend seriously reading or meditating on God's word. You begin to get the picture.

Meditation on God's word is not lying on your back and letting your mind wander as it pleases. It's hard work. It's the effort put forth to take each part of God's word and examine yourself and your life by it. It is seeking to apply God's word to every facet of your life that it may be brought into conformity with the will of God. This demands your complete attention and greatest effort. But it's worth it for the child of God.

The psalmist describes the result in the life of the believer and then contrasts that life with the wicked (the one who refuses to listen to God).

The life of the child of God, molded by God's word, will be like a tree planted (actually transplanted) by the life-giving streams of God (his word, the word of life).

He will be like a tree bearing fruit to the glory of God which will not wither and fade away as all the dreams of this world surely will.

He will prosper in God's sight, though so far as the world is concerned he may seem to have wasted his life—gaining little of what the world calls treasures.

In stark contrast the wicked is lifeless and has no stability. Like chaff in the wind he will be blown about by every wind of doctrine and amount to nothing, in God's sight.

In the end, the day of judgment, only God's children will endure, while those who have sought to live without concern for God or his will shall perish.

Lest we become proud we are reminded that we survive, not because we are better than the rest in our own strength, but because the Lord has known us (chosen us) as he did Abraham and made us different for his own glory.

Nations in Rebellion

Read Psalm 2:1–5 and answer the following:

1. What is the preoccupation of the nations of the world?

_____

_____

2. How does God deal with these nations?

_____

_____

As we learned from Daniel, in God's view all the nations of this world are in continual rebellion against the Lord and his kingdom. They rage against God and meditate things that are vain—the foolishness of this world noted in Psalm 1:1. What they desire is to break with God altogether and live without reference to him. In the Bible this is reflected in Adam's own rebellion. He followed the counsel of Satan, who convinced him that he didn't need to hold to God's word but could be like God—making his own free decisions, unencumbered with God's will.

Throughout Scripture we see this rebellion re-enacted. At Babel those aspiring to build the great tower did not consult the Lord at all but proceeded to put together their ideal world without him. In the end they did not succeed. The Jews sought to do the same in Jesus' days on earth. They didn't succeed either.

75

To this day, though men have often tried, they have not been able to unite the world. If they should ever succeed we can be sure it wil be on a basis that is against God. Have you ever heard Jesus Christ honored by the United Nations?

In our own day we listen in vain for any recognition of God and his sovereignty over the affairs of men by the media or leaders in our society or in any other society.

Yet God is sovereign over men. The psalmist declares this, saying that while men plot to leave God out of their lives God laughs. He laughs at their attempts to live without him. He laughs and warns them in his wrath that he will surely judge them.

As we noted in another chapter, the whole world stands under the judgment of God. It is impending and will surely come. The wicked will perish—all whose lives leave God out or who seek to relegate God to a very insignificant part of their lives.

The Mission into the World

As we have learned already, God, while holding the world under judgment, in his mercy has also done something to prepare the way for calling out of the world those whom he has chosen to be his own forever.

Read Psalm 2:6–9 and answer the following questions:

1. Whom has God set over the nations of the world?

_____

_____

2. What has he given to him?

_____

_____

3. What will he do to the nations?

_____

_____

Just as we saw in the dream of Nebuchadnezzar (Dan. 2) the Lord will not sit back and let the nations of this world have their way. They will ultimately be overthrown. The means of overthrow will be the establishing of the kingdom of God by his own son, Jesus Christ (cf. Acts 13:33; Heb. 1:5; 5:5).

God's only begotten son (the only son of man born into the world as the Son of God) will establish his kingdom on earth and rule the nations of the world, guiding human history until he has brought all history to its conclusion.

Jesus has a mission 'and that mission is to redeem out of the world all whom the Father has given him, as we noted in our first chapter. He must go to the uttermost parts of the earth to reach and claim them. And he has determined, as we have already seen, to do this by sending God's children—already saved—into the world to be his witnesses. They must claim the rest out of every generation in time, out of every part of the earth, in the name of Jesus Christ.

The reason why the nations of this world will all be broken in pieces like a potter's vessel—as Daniel taught Nebuchadnezzar—is that there is no room in God's plans for more than one kingdom: his own.

As we study history we see that the most important aspect of history is what Christ is doing through his people on earth calling men to himself.

We see the world worrying about men destroying themselves by nuclear weapons and scurrying to bring about some kind of peace to prevent it. But in fact the world will not end until God is ready. And when he is ready it *will* end, not by what men do but by what the Lord will do on the last day of human history on earth.

Again we see why it is not our mission to become involved in the world's efforts to save itself. Our mission is to give ourselves fully to the task of rescuing from a world already under judgment those whom the Father has given to the Son. If we become sidetracked by listening to the world's views of what is important today (disarmament, peace treaties, conquest of disease and poverty, etc.) we will utterly fail in our mission.

The psalmist rightly understood the significance of establishing the kingdom of God in the midst of the kingdoms of this world.

The Call to Reconciliation

Read Psalm 2:10–12 and answer the following:

1. Why do you think the psalmist addresses the kings and judges of earth?

_____

_____

2. What does he call them to do?

_____

_____

3. What is the urgency of reconciliation between those of this world and God's son?

_____

_____

4. What is the only refuge for sinful men?

We see from the words of verse 10 that to be wise is to be instructed (in God's word). The psalmist (child of God) challenges kings and judges because God is challenging the kingdoms and leaders of this world—setting up his own kingdom here.

The clear message of the missionaries from Christ to the world is that men must be reconciled to God's son: serve him and rejoice before him or perish.

Kissing the Son means making peace with God through him.

This call is urgent. Impending for all men in the world is the wrath of God. It awaits all at the end of human history, and if men are not reconciled to him now before it is too late they will surely perish.

The alternative is to take refuge in the Lord—in God's son. Again we see that we're on a rescue mission, calling men out of the world to him.

If the church becomes involved in the world's mission— seeking hope in the world and improving man's condition on earth—it will all be in vain, like putting a fresh coat of paint on a ship that's sinking.

What we ought to be doing is getting men off the sinking ship and into the life boat (Jesus Christ)—the only refuge and hope for the world. Do we really believe that?

We have gone halfway through this study. In the Psalms and the rest of the Old Testament we find much more about God's mission into the world. But we cannot give further space to Old Testament study of missions. We go next to the New Testament to see how the Lord has built on what he has taught so far.

Review Questions

1. How does Psalm 1 show the two possible destinies of men?

_____

_____

2. Who is the enemy of the nations of the world?

_____

_____

3. What mission did the Father give the Son according to Psalm 2?

_____

_____

4. According to Psalm 2, how do believers become involved in Christ's mission?

_____

_____

Discussion Questions

1. Describe a life that pleases God in accord with Psalm 1.

_____

_____

2. How is the "chaff" nature of lost men seen today?

_____

_____

3. How is our own nation in rebellion against God and Christ?

_____

_____

4. How can we demonstrate Christ to the world as its only refuge?

_____

_____

7

JESUS' FAMILY: THE CHURCH— MATTHEW 16:15-19

In the Old Testament studies on missions we saw the purpose of God—to have a people to be his forever—carried out in the framework of the family.

We see the same thing as we go to the New Testament.

When Jesus was confronted by those who spoke of his family in terms of his literal mother, brothers and sisters—members of his family in Nazareth—he responded that his true family consists of all who do the will of his Father who is in heaven (Matt. 12:48, 49).

This is in full accord with what we learned about Abraham and his true seed. It was not the seed that came from him physically but the seed that was the result of a faith like his. The true seed of Abraham, and therefore of God, is the result of faith, as with Abraham and every other child of God from the beginning.

Jesus reiterates that principle, declaring that fleshly descent does not count so far as his true family is concerned. What counts is who believes as Abraham did and who shows that faith by obedience to the Father in heaven.

These alone are the family of God and it is within that family alone that the Lord will carry out his purpose to have a people to spend eternity with him. That family is called the church of Jesus Christ.

Building Christ's Church: The Work of Missions

Read Matthew 16:15–19 and answer the following:

1. How was Peter able to make an acceptable profession of faith in Jesus Christ?

_____

_____

2. What is the rock on which Jesus intends to build his church?

_____

_____

3. Where will Jesus build his church?

_____

_____

4. How will the church (true believers) be involved in church building?

_____

_____

5. How will what they do on earth relate to what God in heaven wills to be done?

_____

_____

About halfway through his ministry Jesus called the disciples aside and asked them directly what they thought about him. He did this to show that being his disciples involves more than simply following him around. There must be decisions and commitments and knowledge based on faith if men are to be Jesus' followers.

The time had come for his closest followers to fish or cut bait.

Peter was presumably answering for most of the rest. His profession of faith was clear and brief: You are the Christ, the Son of the living God.

By this profession he was saying that Jesus is the Lord—he is God come into the world to save men, as he had promised in the Old Testament.

That profession is the hallmark of true Christianity. Paul said the same thing when he declared that if we believe in our heart that Jesus is Lord and confess with our mouth that God raised him from the dead we shall be saved (Rom. 10:9).

If you do not believe Jesus is the God who revealed himself in the Old Testament as the Lord and savior of his people you cannot be saved. If you do not believe Jesus is God you have cut the heart out of the gospel message.

Peter affirmed that he believed this, and for that reason his profession was well-pleasing to the Lord.

Yet Jesus was quick to inform Peter that his ability to make such a profession was not from his own power but by the grace of God. Flesh and blood refers to human ability.

As we are born into this world we are born as fallen men— unable to do anything in our own strength to please God. As Jesus explained to Nicodemus, we must be born again by the Holy Spirit if we are ever to see or be able to enter God's kingdom (John 3:3–6).

Jesus understood this and took great comfort in the knowledge that all those whom the Father had given him would surely come to him (Matt. 11:25–30).

Returning to Matthew 16, Jesus was not saying he would build his church on Peter or on any other man. The rock of which he spoke was himself whom Peter, by making the good profession, had recognized as his only savior.

Paul taught the same thing: there is no other foundation for the church than Jesus himself (1 Cor. 3:11). As he preached Christ in Corinth he laid that foundation for the church there (1 Cor. 3:10). That is the way the church must always be built —not on men but on Christ, the true foundation.

Peter fully understood this. In his own epistle he writes of Christ as the true cornerstone of the church (1 Pet. 2:4–6).

Jesus, speaking of building his church so that the very gates of hell could not withstand it, undoubtedly had Psalm 2 in mind. There God clearly gives the authority to his son to invade the kingdoms of this world and establish his own church by calling men out of the world into the kingdom of God.

This gives a clear picture of what missions is all about. It is Christ's invasion of the world, the domain of Satan, to establish his own kingdom and claim out of the kingdoms of the world a people to be his forever.

And how does Christ purpose to do this?

The keys of the kingdom (the way of admittance to the kingdom) will be given to the true church of Christ.

What they do on earth will be done in heaven. He speaks of binding and loosing. To understand this we must see how Jesus conceived of his own mission when he was sent from the Father.

Read Matthew 12:24–29 and answer the following:

1. How did Jesus identify Beelzebub?

2. With whom did the enemies of Jesus accuse him of being allied?

3. What was the fallacy of that contention?

_____

_____

4. What did Jesus say was the significance of his casting out demons?

_____

_____

5. How did he link that particular work to his whole mission?

_____

_____

As Jesus' enemies increased in their determination to stop him at any cost they carelessly accused him of being in league with the devil (the term Beelzebub was one of many terms in use in that day for Satan). Jesus refuted this, showing that it was not true.

If their assumption was true, they would have nothing to worry about because Satan would be opposing himself. But if they were wrong, they should know that Jesus' presence meant the kingdom of God was now among them.

Jesus came not to serve Satan but to oppose him. The casting out of demons was proof that Jesus had power over Satan and could and would set men free from him. He spoke of entering Satan's house (the nations of the world) and binding him so that he could spoil his house. Thus Jesus would bind Satan and at the same time loose those held in his captivity, setting them free to follow Jesus.

Returning to Matthew 16 we learn that what Jesus had seen as *his* mission in chapter 12 he now made the mission of the *church*. Jesus is going to work through the church as it proclaims his gospel (the keys of the kingdom). By its work he will set free from Satan's clutch those held so long in his control. At the same time, he will bind Satan so that he will be helpless to prevent any of those whom the Father has given the Son from being saved.

Jesus certainly was not saying he was giving to the church the authority to decide who would and who would not be saved. But he was saying that what we do on earth as his church proclaiming the gospel is what God wills to be done in heaven. What we do on earth as Christ's church matters to God. It is his work.

As we do his work great things happen. Satan is bound and unable to keep any of those whom God calls to himself. At the same time, as men hear the gospel through the church's preaching and witness they are set free from sin, death and Satan and enter into God's kingdom with us.

Christ: The Sustainer of His Church

Read Matthew 18:15–20 and answer the following:

1. What is the common bond that joins this passage with Matthew 16:15–19?

_____

_____

2. What is the Lord calling for in this passage?

_____

_____

3. What do these two passages (Matt. 16 and Matt. 18) tell us about how Christ intends to work in the world?

_____

_____

The common element in the two passages is the promise that what the church does on earth will be done in heaven. It is true in relation to the work of the church in proclaiming the gospel and also in relation to the work of the church in maintaining the purity of the church.

The only two passages in all four Gospels where Jesus speaks of his church (*ekklesia*) by name are these two (chs. 16, 18). Yet in the subsequent writings of the New Testament the term is used numerous times of the church of Jesus Christ.

This says a great deal, does it not? In these two passages Jesus defines the church and declares that it is through the church he will work—and *only* through the church. That is his decision.

For that reason he not only calls the church to a true profession of faith in him and a full involvement in his work but also to maintain its purity. True proclamation and true discipline (maintenance of purity in testimony and work) are entrusted to the church *only*.

We will not be able to explore the full meaning of discipline in the church, but suffice it to say that discipline involves not simply rooting out sin and dealing with it but also careful teaching of the word and training of the members in that word. It further involves restoring in love those who have been disciplined because they wandered away from Christ's purpose in the church.

This ought to raise serious questions in our minds about the practice of entrusting the work of the church to those organizations which are not the church and which do not maintain discipline.

Every work of the church ought to be carried out by those to whom the Lord entrusted it: those members who have made a true confession of faith in Jesus Christ and who are under the discipline of the church in the work they are doing.

Why the church and not some voluntary (parachurch) organization? Because Christ has determined to work through his church. Where true profession of faith and true discipline as established by Jesus Christ have not occurred, there is no church—just a human organization, no matter how sincere or worthy its cause may seem.

We have seen that the focus of attention moves from the family of men to the family of Christ—his true church.

Within the family of believers the individual families continue to have a vital part in preparing for and carrying out missions, but the work of missions must be channeled through Christ's church—his chosen instrument for proclaiming the gospel to the world and claiming out of the world all whom the Father has given him.

Review Questions

1. How does Christ intend to build his church?

_____

_____

2. What does Christ mean by binding and loosing?

_____

_____

3. What do Matthew 16 and 18 have in common?

_____

_____

4. What is the the problem with missions done outside the church?

_____

_____

Discussion Questions

1. When did the church first appear in human history?

_____

_____

2. How does the Roman Catholic interpretation of Matthew 16 differ from what we have said in this lesson?

_____

_____

3. What part of your church's work is done through para-church groups?

_____

_____

4. What does discipline in the church include?

_____

_____

8

MISSIONS: A FAMILY AFFAIR — MATTHEW 28:18–20

From the beginning of this study we have sought to show that the whole work of missions is family-oriented. It began in the family of God: the Father, the Son and the Holy Spirit. From there came the plan to have an increased family of God, created in the image of God and in his likeness.

When men sinned the process of calling together God's family began—as first planned—in Christ.

The Lord initiated his continuing work among men by establishing the family of Abraham and giving that family the task of being God's people in the world, reaching out to the world with God's message.

The Lord never veered from his purpose to call his family out of the nations of the world. He established Abraham's family to be the means of carrying out that purpose.

When Jesus came into the world he enlarged the concept of his family by showing that not those who were descendants of Abraham according to the flesh but those who were of the same faith as Abraham were Jesus' family—the church.

He established the church as the means of reaching the world for Christ and promised to work through the church, and only through the church, to complete the task the Father gave him: to claim everyone of those given him by the Father.

We see that the Lord has moved from the individual family to the church as the chief means of preparing men for the mission of Christ. But the church is only an extension of the family, which is still the basic unit of the church.

We see this when we look at the Great Commission of Jesus Christ given near the end of his earthly ministry.

The Family-Church Task in Missions

Read Matthew 28:18–20 and answer the following:

1. How is the task of the church like the task given Abraham in his family?

_____

_____

_____

2. How is the sign of baptism like the sign of circumcision given to Abraham?

_____

_____

3. What place does teaching have in the home and in the church?

_____

_____

_____

At last we come to the Great Commission, as it is commonly called. We should see that it is grounded on what we have already learned about missions from the Old Testament.

The very authority by which Jesus speaks at the beginning of the Great Commission is anchored in the words of Psalm 2. Jesus declares that he is taking the authority given him by the Father in that Psalm.

He addresses his church and commissions his disciples to go into the world as the Father first sent him.

The task he gives his church is as he described it in Matthew 16: to make disciples out of all the nations. Remember, he gave the church the keys of the kingdom. What the church does will be the carrying out of what he has determined in heaven. The church is doing his work.

The church makes disciples from all the nations by two particular acts: *baptizing* them into the name of the triune God and *teaching* them to observe all that Jesus has taught. These are the major responsibilities of the church.

These two commands (tasks) relate closely to what the Lord originally taught Abraham to do in respect to his own family.

The church has long recognized the relationship between the

sacrament of circumcision given to Abraham in the Old Testament and the sacrament of baptism given to the church in the New.

God gave the sacrament of circumcision to Abraham when he was making known his great purpose for Abraham and his family. Circumcision—to be given to the household of Abraham—was a sign that the circumcised were under his spiritual care. Anyone not circumcised was considered no part of the family of Abraham (Gen. 17:14).

Circumcision did not guarantee that one was a child of God. Both Ishmael and Esau were circumcised but were later shown not to be part of the true family of God (Abraham's true seed). Circumcision showed that it was Abraham's responsibility to watch over their spiritual lives—to teach them as God had instructed him in Genesis 18:19.

The purpose of circumcision was to remind the circumcised and the circumciser that here was one in need of the grace of God—the cleansing of God—in his heart. It was the responsibility of the circumciser to teach him the way of the Lord—whether or not he ever believed.

God made clear through Moses that what he demands is a circumcised heart (Deut. 10:16). But man cannot cleanse his own heart, let alone the heart of another.

Therefore the Lord promised that *he* would circumcise the hearts of his people (Deut. 30:6). Only by the Lord's work—rebirth in the heart—can men truly become the children of God. You must be born again.

We gain the proper understanding of baptism from this. The

responsibility of the head of every family in the church is to see that all his children are baptized. This does not mean they are saved by that act but that he acknowledges their need of the cleansing work of regeneration which only the Lord can do.

The parents of infants brought to be baptized acknowledge their child's need of the cleansing blood of Jesus and promise that they will faithfully raise their children in the nurture and admonition of the Lord. Baptism, like circumcision, points to that washing of regeneration needed (Titus 3:5–7).

In the Great Commission we see this command expanded beyond the believing family to the church, the parent of all who come to learn the gospel.

All who hear the gospel and respond by making a profession of faith are thereby brought under the instruction of the church. When adults receive baptism the church, by baptizing them, recognizes that these have come under its care—a child born into the family (the visible church)—and are to be taught the word of Christ. True faith comes by hearing the word as God works his grace in the hearer.

The church cannot assume when it has baptized professing adults that they are now truly saved and its task in respect to them is done, any more than parents whose children are baptized can assume that their children are truly God's children.

The continuing work of the church is teaching its children (members) to observe all things that Christ has taught. By that teaching, Christ's word (the whole word of God) will bring to true faith those whom he has called to be his own.

Jesus' parable on the sower and the seed shows that not all

who say they believe really do believe. The church cannot assume any is saved. Only God knows that.

From this we see that the primary task of the church, and therefore of missions, is to continue to teach those who have responded to the gospel, never assuming that this task is finished until Christ returns.

This means that the primary task of any individual church or denomination is to instruct thoroughly those put in its care —its children of all ages who are either brought by believing parents or have, as adults, made professions of faith in Jesus Christ. The church dare not assume that any of these is saved and therefore not in need of further instruction.

Jesus calls the whole process of baptizing and teaching "making disciples." We need to understand that term.

What does it means to *be* a disciple?

Being Christ's Disciple

There is no one text to which we can go to learn what it means to be a disciple. We will look at various passages.

Significantly, the first occurrence of the term "disciple" in the New Testament is Matthew 5:1. The term designates those who were following Jesus and had shown a desire to learn from him.

He took them aside to instruct them (5:2). What he taught is laid out in the next three chapters (Matt. 5–7). It is known as the Sermon on the Mount—really a lesson, not a sermon in the modern sense of that term.

Study of that lesson will give some idea of what is involved in being a disciple of Christ—what the Lord expects of his disciples.

From beginning to end Jesus teaches the word of God, showing its meaning and application in the lives of those who would be God's children.

As he closes Jesus points out that those who would be his disciples must both hear and do these words (Matt. 7:24-27). When he finished, the disciples recognized that his teaching was unique.

Therefore a disciple is one taught by Jesus Christ. That is the chief component of discipleship. But the teaching must lead to obedience—teaching that is lived out in those same disciples.

As Jesus taught elsewhere, they will prove to be his disciples if they remain in his word (continue to learn and obey it, John 8:31). He also taught that others would know they were his disciples if the teaching issued in their loving one another (John 13:35).

A disciple is the disciple of *Jesus Christ* first and always. The current concept that discipling is a matter of what some call "one on one"—my choosing one or two and spending much time with them, instructing them as I have understood the Bible—needs to be re-examined in the light of Scripture.

Discipling in the first place is not the task of individuals but of the church. Jesus did not say to individuals, "Make disciples." He said to the church, "Make disciples."

It is dangerous to suppose that we can isolate one person

and successfully teach him. Our own understanding may be very faulty. God requires the balance he has given to the whole church body, working together, to disciple others properly (Eph. 4:1–16).

In the book of Acts we see clearly that the disciples were not disciples of men but of Jesus Christ (Acts 9:1). Those under the instruction of the word in every church were the Lord's disciples: in Damascus (9:19); in Jerusalem (9:26); in Iconium (13:51, 52); in Derbe (14:20) and in Galatia and Phrygia (18:23).

Because they were the Lord's disciples and not men's, true disciples were challenged to commitment to the Lord alone.

Jesus designated those disciples who did the will of his Father to be his true family (Matt. 12:49, 50). He expected all his disciples to recognize that the new family superseded all other family ties on earth. He called his disciples to love him more than their parents *or* children (Matt. 10:37–39; cf. Luke 14:26, 27).

Their commitment to Jesus meant they were willing to lose their lives for his sake. They were to relinquish all claims on their lives so that they might live for him alone.

This meant his disciples must be prepared to suffer with him as well (Matt. 10:24–33). All the evil thoughts and plots against Jesus would fall on his true disciples. If they were not willing to accept that, they were not fit to be his disciples.

We conclude that to be a disciple of Jesus is to sit under his instruction, learning from him all through one's life—a task more important than any other work. It also means being will-

ing to commit one's whole life and service to him, willing to
suffer with him, sharing in the shame and onus of the cross in
this world—whatever the cost personally.

Making Disciples for Christ

Read Acts 2:37–47 and answer the following questions:

1. How were people enrolled in the school of Christ to be discipled?

   _____

   _____

2. How were they discipled?

   _____

   _____

3. How was it evident that they became truly Christ's disciples?

   _____

   _____

4. How were they saved?

   _____

   _____

There are clearly four stages of discipleship seen in this passage, in accord with what we have already learned.

First, when the word had been preached those who responded were, with their children, enrolled in the school of Christ by baptism. It did not mean they were saved but that they were now recognized to be the charges of the church in Jerusalem—its children.

Second, they were immediately put under the apostles' instruction—taught the word. In the context of this teaching the church gave them fellowship with other disciples. It also offered them the sacrament of the Lord's Supper (breaking of bread) and supported them in the prayers of the church.

Third, the evidence that they were learning to be not just hearers of the word but doers is that they were ready to consider all they possessed to be the Lord's. They showed commitment to the Lord and to one another by fellowship both in the temple and at home. They shared what they had in loving hospitality.

Finally, as this was going on in the church God called from among them those who were to be saved. Thus Jesus was claiming out of this visible church those whom the Father had given him. Faith came by hearing, and hearing by the word of Christ.

This was a mission-minded church; and because it was it produced mission-minded churches, as we shall see in the next chapter.

Here we see the church obeying the Great Commission faithfully: making disciples. It did this by proclaiming the gospel and calling men to believe. Then it baptized those who responded, putting them in the school of Christ—teaching them to observe all things—all that the Lord had taught them.

Review Questions

1. What task has Christ given his church?

_____

_____

2. Compare the sacraments of circumcision and baptism.

_____

_____

3. What does it mean to be Christ's disciples?

_____

_____

4. Who makes disciples?

_____

_____

Discussion Questions

1. Compare Genesis 18:19 and Matthew 28:18–20. How are they similar? Dissimilar?

_____

_____

2. Discuss the similarity between the task of parents in the home and the church's task.

_____

_____

3. What is the problem with "one-on-one" discipling?

_____

_____

4. How is your church making disciples?

_____

_____

9

PORTRAIT OF A MISSION-MINDED CHURCH — ACTS 11:19-30

We have seen the kind of church God raised up in Jerusalem after Jesus had taken his place at the right hand of the Father. We will now look at one of the churches Jesus established among the nations, working through his people. It is important to see that faithful churches produced faithful churches, working hand in hand with the Holy Spirit whom Jesus sent to be his presence with his church until he returns.

Christians in Antioch

Read Acts 11:19-30 and answer the following questions:

1. What caused the believers in Jerusalem to scatter from that city?

_____

_____

2. What unique thing did some of the believers begin to do in Antioch?

_____

_____

3. How were their efforts blessed?

_____

_____

4. Why was Barnabas sent to Antioch?

_____

_____

5. Why did Barnabas go get Saul?

_____

_____

6. What evidence is there that the church members in Antioch became sincere believers?

_____

_____

In the verses preceding this passage we read that Peter, a leader of the church in Jerusalem, learned that the Lord intended the church to break its ties to Judaism and go out to the Gentile world to preach the gospel.

At first the Jewish Christians—virtually all Christians at this point were Jews—preached only to Jews. But some, their memories fresh with the words of Peter about God's intent to reach the Gentiles, began to witness to Gentiles (Greeks) in the

Gentile city of Antioch.

The message to the Gentiles was no different from what they had been preaching: Jesus is the Lord (God). They called men to be reconciled to him.

The Lord showed his approval of their boldness by blessing their efforts. A large number believed and turned in faith to the Lord. This blessing indicated that the grace of God was in that effort.

Barnabas, a man of commitment (4:36, 37) who had befriended Saul of Tarsus (9:27–30), is further described in this text. He was a good man, full of the Holy Spirit and faith. Clearly Barnabas was a sincere believer—living in accord with his profession of faith in Jesus.

The term "full of the Holy Spirit" indicates that believers are not always fully yielded to the Spirit. They may quench him or grieve him.

From the contexts in which the term "full of the Holy Spirit" occurs it seems to refer to the believer's submission to the Spirit's leading. He leads by his word, which he has authored. As one knows that word and is submissive to its teaching he is full of the Spirit—yielded to the work of God through him. Barnabas was this kind of man, and because of that the Lord added many to his kingdom through him.

Apparently Barnabas saw that the task of teaching so many new converts was too great for him alone. He sought help from Saul of Tarsus, whom he had earlier introduced to the Jerusalem church.

Together they continued to teach the church for a year, making disciples not only by baptizing them in the name of the triune God but also by teaching them everything the Lord had commanded.

We have seen that the result of sound teaching ought to be changed lives. When the disciples in Antioch heard of the distress of the brethren in Jerusalem they were ready to give as each had the ability. They sent relief to the believers in Jerusalem suffering under the threat of a great famine.

The Antioch church exemplifies what the Lord expects in his church.

Those who heard the gospel and believed were baptized and brought into the school of Christ. They were taught God's word until they learned to obey it and live by it—doing good works for which they were created in Christ Jesus (Eph. 2:10).

Here we see the Great Commission fleshed out in the membership of one church.

Show me a church which gives attention to the teaching of God's word (and makes that its top priority) and I will show you a mission-minded church.

For them the teaching ministry was the primary ministry and the primary concern. They were doing what Christ expects of his church and this made them a fit base for Jesus to use to reach out farther into the world.

Mission-mindedness and Missionaries

Read Acts 13:1-4 and answer the following:

112

1. What was the context in which the Holy Spirit began to raise up missionaries from the church in Antioch?

_____

_____

2. Who took the initiative in this first mission into the Gentile world?

_____

_____

3. How did the church respond to God's call?

_____

_____

4. Who sent the missionaries?

_____

_____

Jesus laid out clearly and carefully just how he expected his work of missions to be carried on.

First, the church by its prayers must show that it depends wholly on the Lord (Matt. 9:37, 38). It is the Lord's work and not theirs; therefore it must be done his way, not theirs. They are to see the need and then pray that the Lord will do something about it—yielding themselves as Isaiah had done.

Second, it is to be done through Christ's church (Matt. 16:18, 19). As the church is prepared through the teaching of the word of Christ and the people are gathered in prayer, yielded to him, Jesus declares that he will send them out to invade the very strongholds of Satan—the nations of the world.

Third, they are to be responsive to God's lead in mission work. As he raises up from among them those ready and willing to go they are to respond with their full support, sending them in obedience to Christ.

In Acts 13 the two men singled out were sent by the church in Antioch and by the Holy Spirit. The Lord was clearly working his will through his church.

The Scripture says they fasted, prayed and laid their hands on them, sending them away.

Fasting needs more attention. Does it mean they gave up food for a time while they prayed and then sent them away empty to fend for themselves? Not likely!

Read Isaiah 58:5-9. What does God expect with regard to fasting?

_____

_____

Clearly the Lord does not expect fasting to be a mere religious exercise. He shows that what he wants when we fast is for us to give up something that could have been spent on ourselves and use it for God's work: "To loose the bonds of wickedness, to let the oppressed go free, to deal our bread to the hungry and to bring the poor and outcasts to our house."

When that is done our light goes to the world and healing and righteousness go before us—the glory of the Lord accompanying us as we go.

Biblical fasting—what the Lord requires of his people—is sacrificial giving to meet the needs of others. It is giving up our pleasures and making the sacrifice to reach those in the world whom God desires to reach through us. It is giving sacrificially for the work of God!

There was a clear need for support for the work to which God had called that church. The church responded by its fasting (giving up what could have been spent on itself to support the work of Jesus Christ in reaching out to the peoples of the world with his message). We're talking about missionary support from the church—the instrument Christ chose to do his work.

It is sad when missionaries called to service in foreign fields have to spend years going about the church begging for their support. It is not just sad, it is shameful!

It is not right that they should have to beg for such support. The church ought to be fasting: giving up its own pleasures and giving sacrificially to get the word out to the field.

We ought to be ready to say—whenever the Lord raises up another to go—"From what God has given me I will give up my own desires and use it to support his work."

Show me a church whose members are willing to fast—willing to give up their own pleasures and luxuries to support the workers he has raised up in missions—and I will show you a mission-minded church.

A Mission Church

How did the Holy Spirit lead Paul to labor in the world by establishing more churches to be a witness of light in the midst of the darkness of the nations of the world?

Read Acts 20:17–35 and answer the following:

1. What was the curriculum used by Paul in teaching the church in Ephesus?

_____

_____

2. What was his goal in teaching?

_____

_____

3. To what did he commend these spiritual leaders he had trained?

_____

_____

Here Paul tells us more about how he carried out his daily missionary work than anywhere else in Scripture. His life was an open book to the elders he addressed as he prepared to go to Jerusalem after ministering among them.

His curriculum, as he taught among them, was God's word. He taught it in their public assemblies and by visits in their homes. He never veered from that curriculum.

In his own words: "I did not shrink from declaring to you the whole counsel of God." This means he taught all that Christ has taught—the whole word of God revealed in Scripture.

When he had finished his work there, knowing they yet faced many dangers he commended them to God and to the word of his grace. He knew that the only way they could be fully sanctified (fully claimed for Christ) was by remaining in that word—never veering from it.

We have seen that when the church began to witness after Pentecost it began with the teaching of God's word. When churches began to multiply they were stabilized by the teaching of God's word. When they in turn began to grow they were obedient to that word and established other churches among the nations. These too were founded on the word of God, saturated with its curricula, that they in turn might be a light in their area, ever pressing back the god of darkness as they penetrated deeper and deeper into his domain.

The business of a mission-minded church and of a mission church is the same: to teach the word—to make disciples of all those put under its care.

This means that the pulpit time, the other times of instruction—indeed all that the church does—must be centered around the teaching of God's word.

From the pulpit and in the homes Paul preached and taught the word. He knew that only as they knew and were obedient to that word would there be any true mission work in the future.

We shall see how the work done at Jerusalem, at Antioch and at Ephesus is what the Lord will continue to do in his church until he comes again.

Only churches preparing for missions by commitment of time to learn and obey God's word will be used by him in this great work.

Review Questions

1. What was unique about the work at Antioch?

   _____

   _____

2. How did the church at Antioch demonstrate the genuine-
   ness of the faith of its members?

   _____

   _____

3. How did the church at Antioch reduplicate itself elsewhere?

   _____

   _____

4. How were the churches in Ephesus and Jerusalem similar?

   _____

   _____

Discussion Questions

1. Compare the modern view of "full of the Holy Spirit" with
   the view given in this lesson.

   _____

   _____

2. Compare the term "mission-minded church" as it is demonstrated in Acts with the term as conceived by many today.

_____

_____

3. The church at Ephesus was the granddaughter of the Jerusalem church. How many daughter and granddaughter churches has your church produced?

_____

_____

4. Is it planning to do so? What are the problems with daughtering a church?

_____

_____

10

THE GROWING FAMILY — REVELATION 7

When one reads a study of the book of Revelation he tends to swallow and wonder where this will lead. We hope it will lead to a better understanding of the church's mission into the world.

Revelation is a highly symbolic book—its truth is often taught in symbols. Not just any symbols but symbols which have been introduced elsewhere in Scripture. We can understand Revelation's meaning as we understand how the symbols have been used in Scripture. This way great truths of Scripture are brought together in a unique way.

The seventh chapter of Revelation is dramatic. It graphically shows the great tension in the world—in the midst of which the church seems to be working against time—as God saves those whom the Father has given to his Son for an inheritance.

The Great Tension

Read Revelation 7:1-3 and answer the following:

1. What is the tension expressed in this section?

_____

_____

2. What relieves the tension?

_____

_____

3. What does it mean to seal the servants of God?

_____

_____

John, the apostle of Jesus and author of this book, was the last of the apostles to die. Tradition holds that he died in the last decade of the first century.

He relates in the first chapter of Revelation that he was a prisoner on the island of Patmos when the Lord gave him these great truths for the church—the book of Revelation.

In the portion preceding chapter seven John describes the Lamb of God (Jesus Christ), who alone is worthy to rule over history and unfold its meaning. Jesus dominates all human history by his mission into the world to call out a people for his own possession—those whom the Father had given him.

He shows symbolically how history is filled with wars and rumors of wars, social injustice and catastrophic tragedies. All these things seem meaningless to man, so men struggle to correct them. But their efforts are to no avail—all through human history wars, injustice and catastrophes continue no matter how hard man tries to change it.

While men praise those who try to change the world for the

better, only the church, following Christ, is trying to redeem men out of a world under condemnation. And that effort alone is of any lasting value.

Chapter seven opens with a symbolic picture which shows the tension that exists between a world under judgment and the purpose of Christ to redeem his people out of that world before it is destroyed.

The tension is symbolized by four angels holding back the winds of judgment until the work of sealing the servants of God is completed. Indeed the earth cannot be harmed (destroyed) until that work is done.

This tension is expressed many ways throughout Scripture.

In Habakkuk 3:12, 13 the prophet describes God as one who marches through the land with indignation, threshing the nations in anger. But the Lord also goes into the nations to save his people by defeating Satan.

In Psalm 2 the Lord is ready to destroy rebellious men, but before he does he sets up his Son's kingdom on earth as a refuge for all who trust in him.

As Paul put it: The wages of sin is death but the free gift of God is eternal life in Christ Jesus our Lord (Rom. 6:23—cf. John 3:16).

The work of sealing the servants of God noted here has reference to the words of Paul in Ephesians 1.

Paul teaches that we who have heard the gospel and believed have been sealed with the Holy Spirit of promise—the guarantee of our inheritance as the people of God (Eph. 1:13, 14).

The sealing mentioned in Revelation 7:2, 3 pertains to those redeemed and sealed with (indwelt by) the Holy Spirit. The Spirit in them declares that they are God's people: they belong to him (Rom. 8:16), just as we today might put our seal or stamp on a book or other possession to show that it belongs to us.

The tension in the world today as always is between the impending judgment of God on the world—long overdue—and the determination of Christ, through his church, to call out of the world and seal to himself all those whom the Father has given him. The church's work of missions is at the very heart of human history; like a heart, it is what keeps the world going. Without that work in the world it would have been destroyed long ago.

The Multitude

Read Revelation 7:4–12 and answer the following:

1. What is the symbolic significance of the 144,000 sealed?

_____

_____

2. What is the actual number of those sealed?

_____

3. From where do they come?

_____

_____

4. What is the symbol of their having been sealed?

_____

_____

If we read the number 144,000 as a literal number it is frightening: are only 144,000 to be sealed with the Holy Spirit? Is that all there will be in heaven?

Remember, you are reading a highly symbolic book. The question we must ask therefore is: What does the number convey symbolically?

To answer we must look to the immediate context and the general biblical context—what God has taught elsewhere.

In the immediate context we read in verse 9 that John saw a great multitude which no one could number, out of all nations, tribes, peoples and tongues. These are the redeemed of God (vs. 10).

We can conclude therefore that the number 144,000 is not literal but symbolic. What does it symbolize?

The number is the product of 1000 x 12 x 12.

In Scripture 1000 is a frequent symbol for a large but indefinite number, a countless number (Pss. 50:10; 90:4; 2 Pet. 3:8). It is not to be taken literally. It means an unknown but large number.

In the Old Testament 12 was the symbol for the people of God, represented by the twelve tribes of Israel. In the New Testament likewise 12 symbolizes the people of God, the church—the twelve apostles. These same symbols are used in the same way later in Revelation (Rev. 21:12, 14, 17).

The number 144,000 therefore represents the total number of the people of God, no one being omitted. But lest we suppose it is a literal number John is immediately informed that the actual number of the redeemed is countless, in accord with God's promise to Abraham that his seed would be as the stars of heaven in number—impossible for man to count but exactly known by God.

This passage tells us that, when God's work of calling out his own from the nations is done, all will have been claimed and the work completed. A whole family, known to God one by one but to us only as a great multitude.

They are clothed in white, symbolic of those whose sins have been forgiven and who stand righteous in God's sight (3:4, 5, 18; 4:4; 6:11; 7:9, 13, 14).

This is that multitude brought in by the command of Christ given in Matthew 28:18-20—the Great Commission. They are redeeemed and in the presence of God singing praises to God and to the Lamb of God, Jesus Christ.

Through the eyes of John we are able to gain a glimpse of the finished work when the struggle on earth is over; then it will be time to celebrate the great ingathering of Christ's sheep —the eternal day of rest.

It is well to be able to see ahead, to know where we are going. We can know only as God reveals it to us. But contrast our great insight into where we are headed with that of the world which has no such hope. Surely it ought to stimulate us with a greater motivation to work harder in this world, redeeming the time, for the time is short.

Here we are able to see the expanding family of God to its completion. What began as one person, Jesus Christ, shall expand to include every one of those given the Son by the Father, all of his brothers and sisters from all time.

But that expansion of God's family does not come easily. It involves trials and hardships—as Paul told the Ephesian elders: serving the Lord with all lowliness of mind, and with tears, and with trials . . . (Acts 20:19).

The Great Tribulation

Read Revelation 7:13–17 and answer the following:

1. What is the great tribulation?

_____

_____

2. What happens during that tribulation?

_____

_____

3. What is promised in the end?

_____

_____

It is tempting to let our thoughts run wild in such a passage as this and assume it is talking about some particularly difficult time in church history, when some in the church will suffer much more than most Christians in the past have suffered in their life and ministry.

Yet again we must remember that the book is symbolic and conveys its truth by symbols. We need to determine what the great tribulation is, not by our imagination or false assumptions but by God's word.

Jesus speaks of the tribulation that comes on believers as he describes the period of the evangelization of the nations of the world. It is called a period of tribulation and comes during the period the gospel is going out to the world (Matt. 24:4–14). In John 16:33 Jesus tells his disciples that in the world they will have tribulation but to be of good cheer because he has overcome the world.

In both passages it is clear that the tribulation is the whole period of the gospel being proclaimed on earth and the whole period of the church's mission ministry to the nations. As Paul said, it is a time of tears and trials. But it is also the time of men coming to know Christ as savior, of being washed clean in the blood of the Lamb—hence their white garments.

In the world the church will do its work under difficult circumstances: it will not be easy. But it is precisely through that work that men are redeemed out of the world. That is what makes the work so very important.

There will be an end. The Lord helps us see this and to have the courage to carry on now in the midst of trials.

He envisions the day when all tribulation will end: the hunger and thirst, the heat and cold, the tears and hurt. It will end one day—a glorious and eternal day—the day God has been preparing us for.

One day, as God purposed before creation, we will be holy and without blemish in God's presence forever.

What are we waiting for? We must redeem the time while it is day—while we have opportunity to be God's instruments for reaching others. Now is the time of salvation for our generation and we are the ones God has put here to get his work done.

The Lord has been holding back his judgment on the world so that we might finish our work of reaching the nations of the world with the gospel. We cannot afford to dillydally.

Review Questions

1. What is the sealing of the saints all about?

_____

_____

2. What is the great tension in the world?

_____

_____

3. How does the number 144,000 symbolize all the redeemed of God?

_____

_____

4. What is meant by the great tribulation?

_____

_____

Discussion Questions

1. Discuss the present times in terms of wars, rumors of wars, social injustice and catastrophes.

_____

_____

_____

2. How is the great tension shown in your church between the urgency of our task and the world's sure destruction?

_____

_____

3. Discuss tribulation in terms of the church's mission into the world today.

_____

_____

4. What are some factors in our world that make it difficult to realize that this world is under God's judgment and ready to be destroyed?

_____

_____

11

THE TALE OF TWO FAMILIES —
REVELATION 12

In the last chapter we saw how God has planned for his family to grow until it is complete. But we must not forget there is another family in the world, under Satan. That family has to be reckoned with as Christ and his family move out into the world to complete the task of missions, bringing in all whom God will save.

This chapter will deal with the existence of the two forces in the world: Christ and his mission versus Satan and his countermission. In the twelfth chapter we will look at the warfare between the two families in greater detail.

Christ and Satan

Read Revelation 12:1–6 and answer the following questions:

1. How does the woman in the vision symbolize the church (God's people)?

_____

_____

_____

2. How do we know the dragon represents Satan?

_____

_____

3. How is the enmity expressed?

_____

_____

4. How do we know the child is Christ?

_____

_____

The symbolism here is not difficult to understand. The woman with the twelve stars in a garland on her head suggests Israel, the people of God in Old Testament times. The sun, moon and stars were seen in a dream by Joseph, indicative of the family of Jacob (Israel—Gen. 37:9).

The birth of a child as the hope of God's people was promised in the Old Testament and reiterated throughout Israel's history (see Gen. 3:15; Is. 7:14; Mic. 4:10).

The dragon with his seven heads and seven diadems clearly suggests the ruler of this world. We are told that the dragon represents Satan, the devil (vs. 9).

Jesus calls Satan the prince of this world (John 12:31). Other similar titles are given Satan elsewhere in Scripture (2 Cor. 4:4;

Eph. 2:2). Hence the crowns.

Satan, poised before the woman, looks threatening. Like a crouching lion he is ready to devour that child when he is born.

This reminds us of the actual events at Jesus' birth. Satan, through one of his servants, Herod the king (the crown again), sought to kill Jesus upon learning of his birth (Matt. 2:13–23).

Like the dragon in John's vision Herod was unsuccessful in his attempts to destroy Jesus.

The child is clearly identified as the one who is to rule the nations with a rod of iron (cf. Ps. 2). As we have seen, that prophecy was fulfilled in the coming of Jesus into the world and his assumption of his place of rule over the nations after he ascended to the right hand of the Father. In the Great Commission he spells out the authority given to him.

Though he was crucified by the hand of Satan's children in the world, he triumphed over the grave and ascended to the Father to take his place at God's right hand. This is indicated in the vision by the child caught up to God and his throne.

As we have seen, Jesus left his church (the woman in the vision) in the world to serve him. Hence the vision portrayal of the woman fleeing into the wilderness where in a hostile environment she is nourished by God (Rev. 12:6).

The time of her trial in the wilderness—a condition she could survive only by the help of God—is given symbolically as 1260 days. This number, together with the like symbols—"forty-two months" and "a time, times and a half-time"—is not designed to give the actual time of the church's ordeal in the world as it carries on Christ's mission. Rather it connotes that in God's mind it is a set time and will come to its completion when he pleases (cf. Rev. 11:2, 3; 13:5; Dan. 12:7; Rev. 12:14).

Jesus made clear before he left the earth that no one knew the exact time. It is in the hands of the Father (Acts 1:7).

The whole vision, in brief scope, gives a picture of the struggle between the heads of the two families: the family of Satan and the family of God. It shows the hostility inherent in that struggle and the enmity of Satan and his children against Christ and his family.

It also shows that our enemy is formidable and that we can't hope to succeed except by the grace of God. The chief target of Satan—since Christ is out of his reach—is the church, that body of believers to whom Jesus entrusted the mission to invade the strongholds of Satan and call out his elect.

Satan Defeated in Heaven

Read Revelation 12:7–12 and answer the following:

1. What was the occasion of Satan and his angels being cast out of heaven?

_____

_____

2. How do we know that Satan was once admitted to God's

presence before Christ came and finished his work on earth?

_____

_____

3. What was the reaction in heaven to the defeat of Satan in heaven?

_____

_____

4. How was Satan's defeat made possible?

_____

_____

5. What does Satan's expulsion mean for us today?

_____

_____

Michael stands, both in the Old and New Testaments, as the archangel who contends against Satan on behalf of God's children (Dan. 12:1; Jude 9).

When Christ finished his work on earth Satan no longer had access to heaven to accuse God's children before the Lord.

To help us understand this we must remember that Satan

did once have access to heaven, as is seen in the days of Job (prior to Christ's coming into the world).

In Job chapters 1 and 2 we read how Satan stood in heaven and accused Job of insincere faith—not being what he seemed to be. God tolerated the accusations and allowed Satan to test his servant Job. In the end Job proved to be of genuine faith and Satan was proved wrong. Nevertheless the accusations were heard in heaven, presumably on the grounds that his sins had not yet been dealt with.

God was willing, in his great longsuffering, to endure such ranting from Satan, anticipating the day when Jesus would finish his work and the mouth of Satan would be shut. Paul speaks of this day and rejoices (Rom. 8:31–34).

Heaven celebrated the overthrow of Satan. He is now confined to earth, the only place where he still has any power.

God's will has been done in heaven. Satan is silenced. He will finally be defeated on earth too after all of God's children have been called and saved.

The victory on behalf of God's children was won by Christ —the shed blood of the Lamb. It has opened the door for God's will to be worked out on earth in human history.

Satan on earth, like a roaring lion, continues to seek whom he can devour. He knows his time is short and makes it his business to make life as miserable as possible for men on earth —especially for God's children.

It is in that short period of the remainder of human history —short from God's perspective though seemingly endless to the church (2 Pet. 3:8–13)—that the church is commissioned by Christ to carry the gospel to the nations. During that time they must make disciples by baptizing those who profess faith in Jesus and by teaching them all Jesus has taught his church: the whole word of God.

Making War with Christ's Brothers and Sisters

Read Revelation 12:13–17 and answer the following:

1. How is the church (woman) helped during this time of warfare on earth?

_____

_____

2. What is Satan's mission during this time of warfare?

_____

_____

3. How does Satan fight the church?

_____

_____

4. Who in the church are the particular targets of Satan?

_____

_____

This vision portrays the earthly struggle of the church of Jesus Christ against Satan as it carries out Christ's mission. The issue has already been settled in heaven. There is no doubt about the outcome. The victory of Christ's church is certain, but it must be worked out in human history. This vision tells about that.

Satan (the dragon) persecutes the woman (the church) who gave birth to the child (Jesus). Since he cannot touch Jesus he seeks his vengeance against Jesus' church in the world. It is a visible and vulnerable church to be sure. Satan watches for every opportunity to hurt the church.

But Christ did not leave his church without help. The reference to the two wings of an eagle and flight into the wilderness remind us of God's calling Israel to himself in the wilderness at the time of the exodus (Ex. 19:4). At that time Israel had perilous enemies behind her and before her. Behind her was the mighty kingdom of Egypt from which they had just escaped; before her was the awesome wilderness where it would be difficult for even a few to survive, let alone several million. The wilderness was a very hostile place for Israel but God sustained his people there for forty years.

The place where the church labors to serve Christ in the world is described as a wilderness.

Satan's mission is to destroy the church, symbolized by his spewing out water to try to carry her away in a flood. He has never been able to succeed and will not.

Nevertheless he continues to oppose all believers—those who keep God's commandments and have the testimony of Jesus Christ.

The book of Acts relates many incidents of believers being persecuted—some even killed—by Satan. The remainder of church history subsequent to that time is full of such records to this day.

This chapter shows that there are still clearly two, and only two, families on earth: the family of God through Christ and the family of Satan (all the rest).

It should warn us that our task of carrying out the Great Commission of Christ in the world will not be easy. The enmity of Satan is deep-seated.

From Satan's perspective, the longer he can prevent the church from finishing its work the longer he has to live in the world. Of course we know he cannot really delay the coming day of judgment, but neither we nor he knows when that day will come.

Every willful neglect on our part to do the work the Lord has laid before us is like a vote for Satan to have his way a little longer in the world. While God will not delay his own time schedule, we will be accountable for our lack of obedience.

In the next chapter we shall see how the warfare is carried on between the two families on earth and what is at stake.

Review Questions

1. What do symbols like 1260 days, 42 months, and time, times, and a half-time indicate?

_____

_____

2. What is the significance of Satan cast out of heaven?

_____

_____

3. Why is the church in mission described as in a wilderness?

_____

_____

4. What is Satan's countermission against the church?

_____

_____

Discussion Questions

1. How do we see Satan as king in the world today?

_____

_____

2. What difference does it make that Satan can no longer accuse believers before God?

_____

_____

3. How is the church in the world today like Israel in the wilderness?

_____

_____

4. Is our church giving comfort and aid to Satan unknowingly? How?

_____

_____

12

THE WARFARE BETWEEN THE FAMILIES —
REVELATION 13, 14

This final chapter before the review will help us see how Satan works through men to accomplish his will against the church and who the real enemies of the church are. We will also see that though Satan is awesome in his strength he is no match for our Lord, in whom we trust and through whom we go to war against Satan.

Satan's Allies: The Nations of the World

Read Revelation 13:1–10 and answer the following questions:

1. Compare Revelation 13:2 and Daniel 7:1–6, 17, 18.

_____

_____

2. What does this beast in Revelation symbolize?

_____

_____

3. What is the duration of the authority of the beast?

_____

_____

4. What is his mission?

_____

_____

5. Who serves the beast?

_____

_____

6. What are the saints called upon to do?

_____

_____

_____

A comparison between this passage and the one from Daniel 7 indicates that the vision of the beast is a vision of the nations of the world which are under the authority of Satan, the god and king of this world. The seven heads and ten crowns further indicate this—kingdoms of the world.

One of the heads, mortally wounded, indicates that down through history though one nation falls another rises to take its place. Jesus once summarized history in this way: Nation shall rise against nation and kingdom against kingdom (Matt. 24:7).

The world marvels that one nation after another rises and dominates. The psalmist noted that they rise against the Lord and his anointed (Ps. 2:1–3).

John tells us that all the nations of the world worship Satan (the dragon) and all the peoples of earth worship the beast and dragon (Rev. 13:4, 8).

We see the subtlety of Satan. Today in many cities of the world there are bizarre sects that call themselves worshipers of Satan. They actually have churches of Satan. The majority of people in the world look and say, "How strange!"

Most people would not classify themselves as worshipers and servers of Satan and look at such groups with repugnance. Yet John says that *everyone* who is not a child of God (whose name is not written in the Lamb's book of life) *is* a worshiper of Satan—a devil-worshiper, if you please!

This should not surprise us. Jesus called those who did not follow him children of Satan, whom they served (John 8:44). Paul reminded the Ephesian believers that we all were once under the domain of Satan, doing his will (Eph. 2:1–3).

John says that the period of authority of the beast (the nations of this world) will be 42 months, the same as the time the church must struggle in the world (wilderness—12:6). This symbolically represents the unknown period of time of the warfare in the world between Christ and his church and Satan and his children—human history to its end.

The mission of the beast under Satan's authority is to make war against the saints, to overcome them—if he can. We are assured however that this cannot happen (1 John 4:4). But Satan will enlist every nation and tribe and people to try to defeat Jesus' believers in the world (Rev. 13:7).

And what is the exhortation to the church under such circumstances? We are not to take up the sword against Satan or his children. The steadfastness (patience) of the saints rests not in their being more powerful with the weapons of this world than unbelievers but in their waiting in dependence on the Lord for Christ to win the victory in his way—by his word.

Though Jesus plainly says here and elsewhere (Matt. 26:51, 52) that believers and the church are not to fight with the weapons of this world, church history records that many times the church has done just this: literally taking the sword to oppose armies of this world.

But even more subtly, the church has often used the ideas and wisdom of this world to carry on the work of Jesus Christ, learning its techniques and goals not from God's word but from the wise of this world—imitating the world.

Our only proper weapon is the sword of the Spirit—the written word of God. With that in hand and with the rest of the spiritual armor of Christ we are to stand against the wiles of the devil (Eph. 6:13–20).

Most of us don't like to think of having enemies, but on reading this we cannot doubt that we do if we follow Christ. Just being in the world as Christ's brother or sister gives us innumerable enemies: everyone who has not believed in Jesus. They are under their father Satan and it is their desire to do his will. His will is to overcome us. Don't forget it!

Satan's Allies: The False Church

Read Revelation 13:11–17 and answer the following:

1. How is the second beast deceptive?

_____

_____

2. How is the second beast like the first?

_____

_____

3. Why does he appear religious to the world?

_____

_____

4. What is his mission?

_____

_____

5. Why is his number 666?

_____

_____

It is not enough that we must have the entire world and its nations as our enemies: Satan fights dirty. He even enlists on his side a fifth column within the visible church, symbolized here by the beast who looks like a lamb but who speaks like the dragon. This is an excellent symbolic portrayal of what we are taught throughout Scripture.

From the time of Cain and Abel we see how two people can stand side by side, ostensibly to worship God. But one is sincere in heart (God's child) while the other is not (Satan's child). God knows the difference but we usually don't—at least not at first.

That's why the rest of the apostles did not know until near the end that Judas, who was "one of them," was really one of Satan's. That's why Jesus pointed out that when two went up to the temple to pray one pleased God and one did not. When two put offerings in the box in the temple one was righteous and the other was not.

The visible church has always been two churches: a true church of believers redeemed by the blood of Christ and a false church of unbelievers who outwardly look religious but who are far from God in their hearts.

The fact that there is a false church makes the task of missions even harder for true believers.

Jesus warned that there would arise false prophets deceiving many—if possible even the elect (Matt. 24:24). John portrays this symbolically by great signs from heaven (like the sign of Elijah, 1 Kings 18—fire coming down from heaven). Symbolically this means that, to most, false Christians will look impressive.

The chief mission of this false church is to enlist all to follow not Christ but the world.

The mark of the beast, as it is often called, is best understood when we study Deuteronomy 6. In this Old Testament passage the Lord was teaching his people to live so that it would be as though God's word were written on their hands and on their foreheads—guided by God's word in all they do and all they plan.

In Revelation 13 we have the countermark of the world on the hands and foreheads of Satan's children. The wisdom of the world and the ways of the world affect everyone who does not belong to Jesus Christ.

God's children, so different from the world, find it extremely difficult to buy and sell and indeed even to live in this world. If they resist the influence of the world and dare to be different—to live like the children of God—just living here will be hard.

The number of the beast, 666, symbolizes what is altogether unacceptable to God—gross imperfection. This is shown by 6-6-6 being continually short of the biblical number for perfection—7.

We learn that Satan has two allies: the nations of the world (all of those living in the world who openly reject the church and live to please Satan); and a false church which, pretending to be the true church, nevertheless lives by the teachings of the world, not by the word of God.

It would be comforting to think that the false churches are limited to those which have openly rejected the Bible and are designated by many as "liberal." But we would only be deceiving ourselves if we thought that. In fact the false church is everywhere: there is no denomination, not a single congregation, that can feel safe from it. It is everywhere that true believers are to be found. Paul even warned the elders of Ephesus that from among them would arise some who are grievous wolves speaking perverse things and drawing away many after them (Acts 20:29, 30).

It would be foolish to ignore this fact when speaking of the great mission of the church into the world.

Nevertheless we cannot afford to be overcome or discouraged by the presence of a false church within the visible manifestations of the church in our day. We have a mission and Christ is in it with us to the end. Woe to us if we quit now!

Christ's True Church and Its Mission

Read Revelation 14 and answer the following:

1. How is Christ and his true church symbolized in verse 1?

_____

_____

2. What is their mission (vss. 6–13)?

_____

_____

_____

3. What are the two harvests and their significance?

_____

_____

There is much in this chapter we will not be able to deal with, but we will focus on a few important points.

In verse 1 Christ and his true church are symbolized by the vision of the Lamb standing with his 144,000. We have already seen that this number is indicative of the whole church of Christ. They are called virgins because the true church is Christ's bride (Eph. 5:24–27; Rev. 21).

Though faced with a hostile world and a deceitful false church the mission cannot be abandoned. The church has been given the everlasting gospel to preach to those who dwell on earth—every nation, tribe, tongue and people (14:6; Matt. 28:18–20).

As we have seen, the urgency of this mission is the impending judgment of God on the unbelievers of the world. Those who worship the beast will feel the full wrath of God—the lake of fire forever (vss. 8–11).

As Jesus looked out over the future history of man he blessed those who follow him, willing to suffer and even die for Christ. They will endure much tribulation but in the end they will rest from their labors. What they have done on earth will endure (vss. 12, 13).

This should stir our hearts to realize that every one of us who is a true believer has been called to follow Christ and to partake in his great mission into the world. We are in the world right now and the world is all around us, preaching its false gospel to all who live here.

We have a true message which alone can change lives and bring others from spiritual death as children of Satan to eternal life in Jesus Christ.

Some of us are called to go to the foreign nations of the world and carry that gospel; others are called to be his witnesses right where we are now—living daily before the world in our jobs and social life. We are *all* missionaries.

The mission of Christ demands all that we are and all that we have. Whatever talents and gifts Christ has given us are for service to him in his mission. Whatever possessions we have are to be given to him freely for sending the gospel to the ends of the earth.

We don't know how much time we have or where the Lord will lead us in this mission, but we ought to know that wherever we are right now we *are* his witnesses—for good or for bad. Let us examine our lives and how we live daily and our bank accounts and what we have that belongs to Christ, and let us give ourselves fully to this mission.

Every minute two harvests are going on in the world. One is described in 14:14–16. It is the harvest Jesus mentioned in the Gospels (Matt. 9:37, 38; John 4:35–37). It is our task to go out into the world and bring in those whom the Father has given to the Son to be his possession forever.

The other harvest is going on too. Every time anyone in the world dies without Jesus Christ he is harvested in the harvest described in 14:17–20. It is the harvest of the wrath of God for those who refuse to believe in Jesus Christ as their savior and for those whom the church never reaches in time.

The fact that not one of those whom the Father has given the Son will be lost does not let us off the hook. If we refuse to be a part of the great commission which Christ has given his church we shall have to answer for it.

Review Questions

1. What does the first beast of John's vision represent?

_____

_____

2. What does the second beast of John's vision represent?

_____

_____

3. What does the number 666 signify?

_____

_____

4. What is the mark of the beast?

_____

_____

5. What do the two harvests signify?

_____

_____

Discussion Questions

1. Discuss ways in which Satan is using the world today to ensnare the church.

_____

_____

2. Discuss various types of devil-worshipers in the world today.

_____

_____

3. What are some evidences of the false church in alliance with the world today?

_____

_____

4. Discuss ways in which we may be poor witnesses for Christ in our daily lives.

_____

_____

13

MISSIONS AND YOU: A REVIEW

In this chapter we will try to make some practical suggestions for getting more involved in the great mission of the church to reach the nations of the world and make disciples out of them for the kingdom of God.

Pray to the Lord of the Harvest

We saw that the beginning of missions was not at the time of the Great Commission but in the council of the triune God before he created man. Missions took as its starting point the will of God to have a people to share the heavenly blessings with him forever.

Central to that plan was the coming of his own Son into the world to make it possible for sinful men to be fit for heaven.

Jesus came into the world with a clear mission: to save those whom the Father had given him out of the world. He began that mission while on earth, giving his life to make them righteous in the sight of God. He directly called a few of those given him by the Father and before he returned to heaven he prayed for them. They were to carry the mission to its completion. He also prayed for those who would believe and be claimed for Christ through the ministry of his church on earth.

As we become involved in missions the first thing we need

to learn is to have the same concern for that mission as Christ had. It was his whole life on earth; it must be ours too.

Following Jesus' example, we must learn to pray without ceasing for the completion of Jesus' mission on earth. As he did, so must we pray for those whom the Father has given him out of the whole world—particularly those living in our day who are yet to be claimed for Christ.

Our prayers must be directed to *his* sending his laborers into the fields of harvest. If such a prayer is to be sincere we and our children must be laid on the line for Christ's service, whether in our own community or in some land far way— wherever the Lord of the harvest wills.

Such prayer is the first involvement of each of us in the work of Christ's mission. If we don't get involved on this level we cannot expect to have much zeal for missions in the long run.

Pray every day that the Lord of the harvest will send his laborers into the fields. Only he can direct them to where they ought to go, only he can put them where they need to be. That means that as we pray we are saying we are willing to be moved to another neighborhood or town or nation to serve him, and that we are willing to reach out to whomever he leads us to right where we are now.

Begin in Your Own Family

We saw how the Lord set a high priority on the family as he created man male and female with a need for each other. The human family simply reflects the eternal family in heaven. Ultimately we must be a part of that family in order to have any part in God's great plan of salvation.

The priority of the family in God's plan means that subjection among the members of the family is essential. Husbands are to make the establishing of a strong Christian home their top priority. First concern must be the needs of their wives and meeting those needs in love.

Each member of the family is to subject himself or herself to the others: wives to husbands, husbands to wives, children to parents, parents to children, in the common cause of making the family strong and well-pleasing to the Lord. Together our family must strive to be all that God wills his children to be: holy, without blemish, in God's presence, in a bond of love.

This is because the family is the first line of defense against the world and its influence if the church is to be strong.

It is also the place where God's people ought to learn the first lessons of going in the way of the Lord (living the Christian life in the world). And it is the first place from which God's children ought to begin to reach out to the world for Christ and his gospel.

Each family is to become a testimony in its neighborhood of the difference Christ makes in the lives of men. This is true whether that believing family is in Sleepy Hollow, U.S.A. or a missionary family on the other side of the earth. If you want to get involved in missions, your family, in your neighborhood, is a good place to begin!

Teaching our children God's word in our homes is very much a part of the Great Commission. Strive to do more than have a devotional. A time ought to be set aside for Bible instruction daily. If we neglect this, all other efforts we may make in missions are mere lip service.

But remember, teaching only in words is not teaching diligently. To teach diligently, as the Lord requires, means to set an example of application of God's word to our own lives so our children can learn to be not just hearers of the word but doers as well.

Witnessing Where We Are:
Beginning in "Jerusalem"

From Isaiah we saw the concept of nations flowing to Zion, and from Zion a people going out to the nations of the world. Isaiah showed himself to be a ready servant in God's mission: "Here am I, send me!" So must we be ready servants.

To begin with, God has already put each of us in the world. Not only in our particular neighborhood and community but in the particular job we have. To despise or overlook the opportunities at hand is to say in our heart that we really are not interested in missions.

We must learn to do our daily job—whatever it may be that the Lord has given us ability to do in our daily work—not as a means of earning a living or as an opportunity to gain raises in salary or promotions before men but as a means of serving Christ. We shall discover that we *are* missionaries already on the front lines of the world.

There is no use in our talking of supporting missions in some foreign field if we are unwilling to be Christ's missionaries where he has sent us already (where he has put us in the world).

If we look around we will see that God has also brought many foreign students to our doorsteps. These are people who for the most part have come to our community without any knowledge of the gospel. But they ought not to go away from us back to their lands without having heard the gospel—without being instructed in God's word.

If you cannot teach them, then make your home a place where others can. Open your home to the opportunity for them to hear God's word as Matthew invited the tax collectors and sinners into his home to hear Jesus.

Dare to be a Daniel, doing what you do in such a way that God is glorified and remembering that your circumstances— where you live and what your job is—are not excuses for not doing Christ's work but opportunities for doing it given you by the Lord of the harvest.

Become Involved in Taking the Gospel
to the Nations of the World

This means becoming involved in your own church's and denomination's work in the missionary enterprise. Jesus Christ made clear that he intends to carry on his work through his church, which he has established.

Jesus called those who believed in him his new family. We all have a new family in the church of Jesus Christ. As we began in our own families we should also broaden our life of service to God in and through his church.

View the church of which you are a member as the channel through which the Lord would use you and your resources in reaching others in the world. Don't look for other channels, use the one Christ has given you.

He gave the Great Commission to the church and not to any other organization. To the church he gave the sacraments: baptism and the Lord's Supper. To the church he gave the authority to proclaim the gospel (the keys of the Kingdom). And to the church he gave the task of making disciples of all nations—including the exercise of discipline—that none of those souls entrusted to the church might be lost and that all might learn to serve God faithfully.

Be involved in all levels of your church's work, for that *is* missions. Be instructed in God's word by those he has placed over you to teach you (disciple you). Be involved in bringing others into that fellowship to be baptized and taught the word of God. Be involved in the work of ministry, sharing what you have with others, that Christian love might be demonstrated among you. Be involved in getting your church involved in its missionary task to reach to the ends of the earth with the gospel, through your mission committee or agency.

Open your home to those foreign missionaries supported by the church when they are home from the foreign field. Learn about the places and people where they labor and learn to pray for them more intelligently.

Pray with your church for the Lord to raise up others to go into the fields of harvest, being willing to go yourself wherever he would lead you. But as you pray examine what the Lord has put into your hands and be willing to *fast* in the biblical sense of that word.

This means taking the possessions God has given you and offering them to the Lord through his church. It means being willing to give up your own plans for what you possess beyond your own needs.

It is hypocritical to ask the Lord to send out others to the fields of harvest when you yourself are unwilling either to go or to make personal sacrifices to support those who do go. Don't let the church—or missionaries sent by the church to other fields—have to ask you for support. Moved by the Holy Spirit through his word, have your gifts ready—indeed, bring them to the storehouse for God's use now.

Become involved in establishing a daughter church from your own. As your church gains members and strength begin to encourage your church to look beyond its own neighborhood to other places where new churches might be established. Be willing to be a seed family, taking your family to another part of your community, into an unreached neighborhood, to begin a new work there.

Fight the Good Fight of Faith in the World

It will not be easy to work with your family to be sound in the faith and knowledgeable of God's word when so many other families even in the church are unwilling to do this. It will be easier to give a little for missions and attend the annual missions conference in your church and let it go at that. That is the common pattern.

Self-involvement, beginning in your own family and neighborhood, is hard when others around you are enjoying the things of this world with their income and time. But it is essential if you are to be a part of Christ's mission.

Don't be surprised if others, even in your own church, ignore the principles of missions you have learned in this study. Remember, you must be guided not by what the majority says or does but by what God's word says.

It shouldn't surprise you that to do Christ's will is hard. Remember, Satan not only has the nations of the world under his control but also a vast false church intermingled with the true believers in this word so that they will not be visibly separated until Christ comes again. That's what you are up against.

Giving time to make your family spiritually strong may not seem as glamorous as going to a foreign field as a missionary but it is just as much a part of Christ's mission into the world.

Giving time and effort to reach the lost next door may not gain the kind of recognition that going to another part of the world gains; but in God's sight the mission field is the whole world, including your own neighborhood.

Giving up some of the luxuries and fleshly indulgences of this world to give what God has entrusted to you for the support of his work may not be the way the world or even many in your own church have gone, but it is what God expects of those who are serious about missions.

Don't expect the approval of men for doing mission work in a biblical way: expect discouragement and opposition. But then remember that you are in a war as Jesus was while on earth. The lines are drawn—have been from the beginning— and at stake are the souls of multitudes yet to be claimed for Jesus Christ.

On every level—in your home, in your church, in your neighborhood, in the nations of the world—today is the time and the whole world is the place. Get involved!